Quilts for Men

from Crib to Dorm to Den

Landauer Books

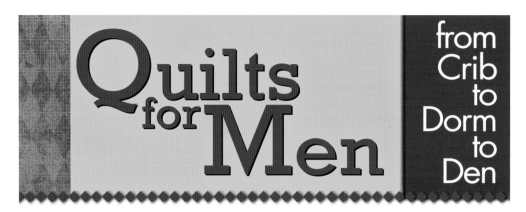

Copyright© 2008 by Landauer Corporation

This book was designed, produced, and published by Landauer Books
A division of Landauer Corporation
3100 101st Street, Urbandale, IA 50322
www.landauercorp.com   800/557-2144

President/Publisher: Jeramy Lanigan Landauer
Director of Sales and Operations: Kitty Jacobson
Managing Editor: Jeri Simon
Art Director: Laurel Albright
Technical Editor: Rhonda Matus
Photostylist: Sue Voegtlin
Photographer: Craig Anderson Photography

ISBN 13: 978-0-9800688-5-6
ISBN 10:   0-9800688-5-1

Library of Congress Control Number: 2008920305

This book printed on acid-free paper.
Printed in China

10-9-8-7-6-5-4-3-2-1

INTRODUCTION

"My daughter just had a baby boy. My son plays football. My husband loves to go camping. My brother just bought a boat. My father is a golfer. Tom leaves for college in the fall."

Sound familiar? These are the events that fill our days with pleasure and promise and give us wonderful reasons—and excuses—to create special quilts for the men in our lives.

You'll find ideas and inspiration from crib to den. Not only are there quilts for every age, but also for a wide variety of interests. Quilters will enjoy the variety of techniques, from traditional piecing, to colorful appliqué and interesting geometrical designs. There's even a beginning primer on painting on fabric.

As you create your new quilt, enjoy the sharing and the awareness that you're about to make your favorite man feel even more special.

The Editors at Landauer

CONTENTS

Teddy Bear Snuggler Blanket

Sheriff Billy Wallhanging

Baby Pinwheel Quilt

Magic Cape

Buggy Nights Quilt

Beach Quilt

Bachelor's Wheel Quilt

Huddle Up Quilt

Patriot Games Quilt

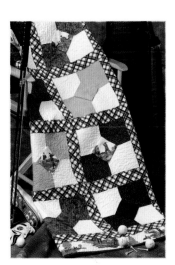

Tee Time Quilt

Fields & Streams Quilt

Nautical Alphabet Quilt

Indian Meadows Wallhanging

GENERAL INSTRUCTIONS

FOR EVERY PROJECT:

Here are some guidelines for gathering your materials for each of the projects in this book:

■ For best results use good quality 100% cotton fabrics. These should measure between 42" and 44" wide.

■ You may have some fabrics on hand for the projects in this book. Fat quarters, 18" x 22" fabric rectangles, are used in many of the projects. Other fabric cuts are listed below:

1/8 yard cut	*= 4-1/2" x 44" rectangle*
Fat Eighth	*= 9" x 22" rectangle*
1/4 yard cut	*= 9" x 44" rectangle*
Fat Quarter	*= 18" x 22" rectangle*

■ You may pre-wash fabrics for these projects, but it is not necessary. It is a good idea to test red and other colored fabrics for bleeding. Place a scrap of fabric in a glass or bowl of hot water. If you see a color change in the water, you may want to pre-wash that particular fabric. You should rinse until the water runs clear, then line or machine dry and press.

■ Use a rotary cutter, acrylic ruler, and self-healing cutting mat to cut fabric strips. Cut the fabric strips into squares, rectangles, or triangles as directed in each pattern.

■ All seam allowances are 1/4" unless noted otherwise.

■ Press seams in one direction following arrows if indicated. If no arrows are indicated, press seam towards the darker fabric.

HAND APPLIQUÉ:

- Using template plastic or freezer paper, trace around each appliqué shape and cut out.

- Draw around template onto right side of desired fabric using pencil, chalk pencil, or washable sewing marker.

- Cut out appliqué 1/4" beyond traced line.

- If layers of appliqué are needed, begin working at the background and work forward.

- Using the drawn line as your guide, slip stitch the appliqué into place. Use your needle to fold under the seam allowance. Take a 1/8" stitch down through the background fabric. Bring the needle up through the fold of the appliqué catching a few threads of the appliqué fabric. Insert the needle as close as possible to where it came up and continue for the entire appliqué shape.

MACHINE APPLIQUÉ:

- Using lightweight fusible web, follow the manufacturer's instructions for tracing and fusing.

- Trace the appliqué shape onto the paper side of the fusible web. Cut the fusible web about 1/8" from the outside traced line.

- Fuse the pattern to the wrong side of desired fabric. Cut out on the traced line.

- Peel off the paper backing. Position the appliqué on the background fabric. Fuse in place. Machine-stitch using a zigzag or buttonhole stitch.

FINISHING THE QUILTED PROJECTS:
LAYERING

- Cut the backing and batting 4" to 6" inches larger than the finished quilt top.

- Lay backing wrong side up on a smooth flat surface. Secure the edges with tape. Center the batting over the backing. Smooth the batting out. Layer the quilt top in the center of the batting. Smooth the quilt top out.

- Baste with large running stitches or small safety pins every 3" to 4". Begin in the middle and work out to the edges.

QUILTING
BY HAND

- Using hand quilting thread; thread a quilting needle with an 18" length of thread. Tie a small knot at the end. Insert the needle through the quilt top and into batting about 1" from where you want to begin quilting. Bring the needle up at the beginning of the quilting line. Give the thread a gentle tug to pull the knot through the quilt top and down into the batting.

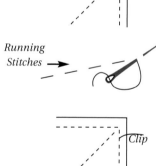

Quilting Patterns

Running Stitches →

Clip

- Take several small running stitches at a time, keeping stitches even and as close together as possible (1/8" to 1/4").

- To end a line of stitching, make a small knot close to the fabric. Insert the needle into the fabric and bring it out again about 1" from the end of the stitching. Pop the knot through the quilt top into the batting and clip the thread close to the quilt top.

BY MACHINE

- Use a walking foot for straight stitching of quilting lines. This will help to keep all layers of the quilt even. Pivot the fabric by keeping the needle in the down position when changing directions.

- Quilting stencils may be used for all types of designs. A free-motion or darning foot is used for this style of quilting.

Adding a Hanging Sleeve

■ A sleeve for hanging is added to the back of the quilt after the quilting has been completed and before the binding is applied.

■ Measure the width of your quilt top and add 2". Cut a strip of fabric 8" wide by your quilt top width plus 2".

■ Fold each of the short edges of the fabric strip under 1-1/2" and press. Sew with a 1/4" seam along each folded edge to hem the sleeve.

■ Fold the sleeve length in half, wrong sides together. Press.

■ Align the raw edges of the sleeve with the top edge of the quilt top. Pin in place.

■ Machine baste the sleeve to the quilt, using a scant 1/4" seam allowance.

■ Add the binding to your quilt.

■ Hand-stitch the folded short edge that lays against the quilt back and the folded long edge of the sleeve to the quilt backing. Be careful that your stitches do not show on the quilt front.

■ If you are planning to display a larger quilt you will want to add more than one hanging sleeve to evenly distribute the quilt's weight.

BINDING
French-fold (double-fold) Binding with Mitered Corners

■ The final step in completing your quilt is to bind the edges.

■ Cut the binding strips for your quilt from selvage to selvage. Sew the short ends of the binding strips right sides together with diagonal seams. Trim 1/4" from the sewn line and press open.

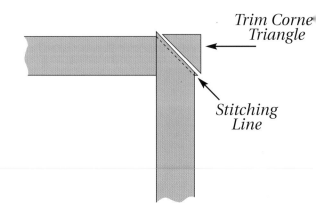

Trim Corner Triangle

Stitching Line

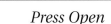

Press Open

■ Fold the binding strips, wrong sides together, in half lengthwise, and press.

■ Fold under a 1/2" hem at the beginning of the binding. Leaving approximately 4" of binding free, begin sewing the binding to the front of the quilt layers at the center on the bottom edge. Use a 1/4" seam allowance. Sew to 1/4" from the first corner, stop, and clip the threads. Remove the quilt layers from under the presser foot.

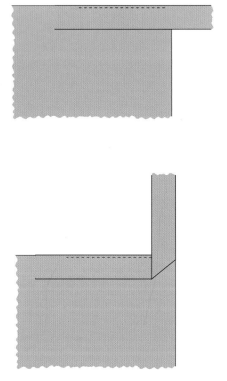

■ Fold the binding strip up at a 45-degree angle, as shown.

■ Fold the binding strip back down upon itself, making sure that the horizontal fold in the binding is even with the top edge of the quilt layers, as shown. Begin sewing the binding to the quilt exactly where the previous seam ended. Continue sewing and repeat at each remaining corner.

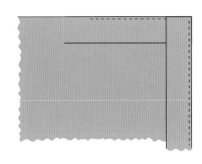

■ To end, slide the end of the binding into the free portion at the beginning. Sew the remaining seam.

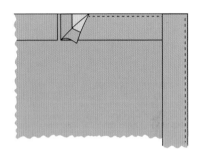

■ Turn the binding over the edge to the backing side of the quilt, and hand-stitch in place. A folded miter will form at each corner; stitch these folds closed.

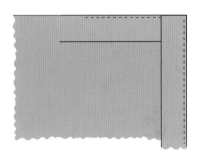

FROM CRIB

Create fun with bears,
cowboys, magicians,
and colorful bugs
in cozy and cuddly
fabrics for favorite
babies and active boys.

blocks

brown teddy bear

teddy bear snuggler

Finished Size:
41-1/2" x 54"

Materials
2 yards of bear-motif fabric for center and appliqués

1-5/8 yards of blue fabric for backing

1 yard of white fabric for border

Lightweight paper-back fusible web

Brown embroidery floss

White perle cotton

Large-eye sewing needle

Yardages are for 60"-wide fabrics.

Cutting measurements include 1/4" seam allowances.

Cutting Instructions
From bear-motif fabric, cut:
  (1) 30" x 43" center rectangle.

From blue fabric, cut:
  (1) 44-1/2" x 57" backing rectangle.

From white fabric, cut:
  (2) 6-1/4" x 43" border strips.
  (2) 6-1/4" x 41-1/2" border strips.

Adding the Border
1. Sew the 6-1/4" x 43" white border strips to the long edges of the 30" x 43" bear-motif center rectangle. Press the seam allowances toward the border.

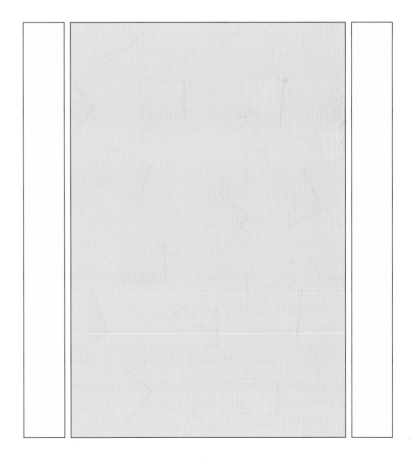

2. Sew the 6-1/4" x 41-1/2" white border strips to the top and bottom edges of the center rectangle to complete the blanket front. Press the seam allowances toward the border.

Adding the Appliqués

1. Cut 10 pieces of fusible web, each slightly larger than the size of an individual bear-motif on the remaining fabric.

2. Center a fusible web piece behind an individual bear-motif on the wrong side of the fabric. Following the manufacturer's directions, fuse the web to the fabric. Repeat to fuse a web piece behind 10 bears. Cut out the motifs, leaving 1/4" around the outside of each bear. Remove the paper from the fusible web.

3. Refer to page 17 to arrange the bears on right side of the white border, keeping the appliqués at least 1-1/4" from the outer edges of the border. Fuse the

appliqués in place. Hand blanket-stitch around each appliqué shape with three strands of brown embroidery floss.

Finish the Blanket

1. Smooth out the 44-1/2" x 57" backing rectangle wrong side up on a large flat surface. Center the blanket front, wrong side down, on the backing; pin-baste the layers together. Refer to the diagram to secure the layers with ties, using a large-eye needle and perle cotton. Trim ends of perle cotton to 3/4" to 1".

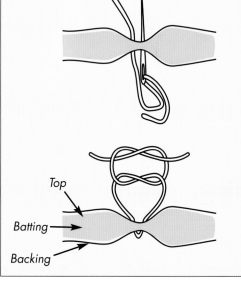

How to Tie a Square Knot
With a single stand of yarn or heavy floss, take a 1/8" to 1/4" stitch through all three layers. Make a square knot - right over left; left over right

Top

Batting

Backing

2. To create a 1"-wide binding, fold the backing edges under 1/2" and then 1". Pin the inner folded edge in place on the front, mitering the backing at the corners. Hand- or machine-sew the folded edge of the backing to the front, mitering the fabric at the corners.

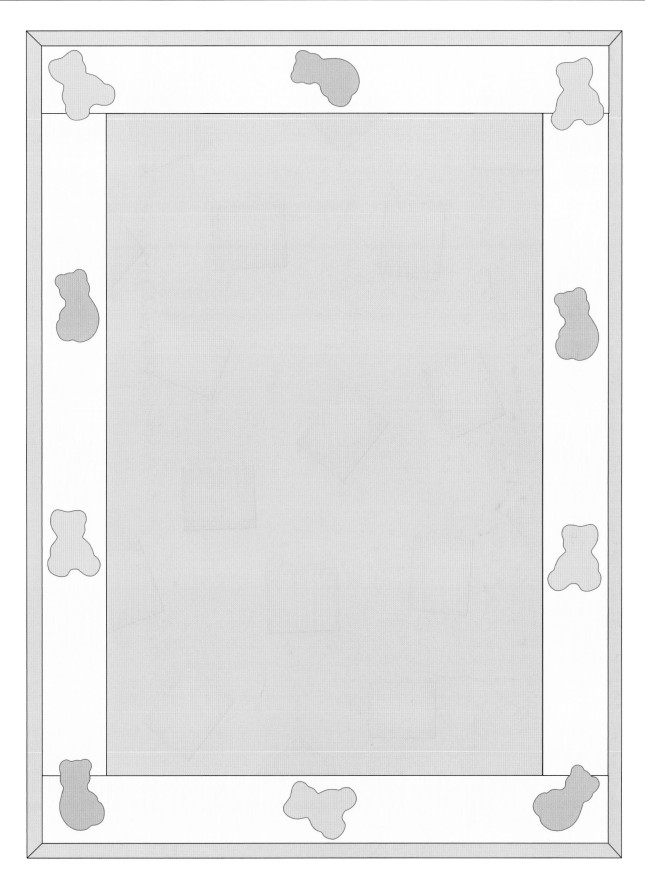

Teddy Bear Snuggler Blanket

baby pinwheel

Finished Size:
45-1/2" x 54"

Block Size:
6" square

Materials
1-5/8 yards of green fabric for blocks, outer border, and binding

1 yard of yellow fabric for background

3/4 yard of print fabric for blocks and inner border

3 yards of backing fabric

52" x 60" piece of batting

Yardages are for 44/45"-wide fabrics.

Cutting measurements include 1/4" seam allowances.

Cutting Instructions

From green fabric, cut:
- (4) 3-7/8" x 42" strips.
  From the strips, cut:
  (40) 3-7/8" half-square triangle squares.
- (5) 5" x 42" outer border strips.
  From the strips, cut:
  (2) 5" x 36-1/2" outer border strips; reserve extra.
- (5) 2-1/2" x 42" binding strips.

From yellow fabric, cut:
- (2) 6-1/2" x 42" strips.
  From the strips, cut:
  (12) 6-1/2" setting squares.
- (2) 6-7/8" x 42" strips.
  From the strips, cut:
  (7) 6-7/8" squares; cut the squares in half diagonally to make a total of 14 setting triangles.
- (1) 7-1/4" square; cut the square into quarters diagonally to make 4 corner triangles.

From print fabric, cut:
- (4) 3-7/8" x 42" strips.
  From the strips, cut:
  (40) 3-7/8" half-square triangle squares.
- (5) 1-1/2" x 42" strips.
  From the strips, cut:
  (2) 1-1/2" x 34-1/2" inner border strips; reserve extra.

From backing fabric, cut:
- (2) 30-1/2" x 52" backing rectangles.

Assembling the Pinwheel Blocks

1. Draw a diagonal line on the wrong side of (40) 3-7/8" print squares as shown.

2. With right sides together, layer the 3-7/8" print squares on the 3-7/8" green squares. Sew 1/4" from each side of the drawn lines as shown.

3. Cut on the drawn line between the stitching as shown. Press the seam allowances toward the green fabric. Check to be sure your half-square triangles each measure 3-1/2" square; trim if necessary.

4. Arrange sets of four half-square triangles as shown. Sew the half-square triangles together in rows and then sew the rows together to make 20 pinwheel blocks.

Make 20

Assembling the Quilt Center

1. Lay out the pinwheel blocks, the (12) 6-1/2" yellow setting squares, 14 yellow setting triangles, and 4 yellow corner triangles on a large flat surface as shown.

2. Sew the blocks and the setting squares and triangles together into diagonal rows, pressing the seam allowances toward the setting squares and triangles. Sew the rows together to complete the quilt center. Press the seam allowances in one direction.

Adding the Borders

1. Sew the 1-1/2" x 34-1/2" print inner border strips to the top and bottom edges of the quilt center. Press the seam allowances toward the inner border.

2. Sew together the 3 remaining 1-1/2"-wide print inner border strips to make one long strip. From the strip, cut (2) 45" lengths. Sew these lengths to the left and right edges of the quilt center. Press seam allowances toward the inner border.

3. Sew the 5" x 36-1/2" green outer border strips to the top and bottom edges of the inner border. Press the seam allowances toward the outer border.

4. Sew together the 3 remaining 5"-wide green outer border strips to make one long strip. From the strip, cut (2) 54" lengths. Sew these lengths to the left and right edges of the inner border. Press the seam allowances toward the outer border.

Finishing the Quilt

1. Sew together the 30-1/2" x 52" backing rectangles along one long edge, using a 1/2" seam allowance. Press the seam allowances open.

2. Layer the pieced backing, the batting, and the quilt top. Baste the layers together and hand- or machine-quilt as desired.

3. Use diagonal seams to sew the 2-1/2"-wide green binding strips together to make one long strip. Sew binding to the edges of the quilt.

4. Trim the extra batting and backing even with the edges of the quilt top. Turn the binding over the edge to the back and hand- or machine-sew in place.

Baby Pinwheel Quilt

Bugs delight—not bite—with this colorful quilt dressed in fun prints, jazzy borders, and whimsical appliqué.

buggy nights

Finished Size:
44-1/2" x 56-1/2"

Materials

8 or more assorted bright print fat quarters for small blocks and appliqués

1/2 yard of white print fabric for appliqué blocks

2-5/8 yards of black fabric for block background and inner border

3/8 yard stripe fabric for small blocks

1/3 yard of yellow print fabric for appliqué blocks

5/8 yard black print fabric for border

3 yards of backing fabric

1/2 yard of turquoise fabric for binding

51" x 63" piece of batting

1 yard lightweight paper-back fusible web

Lightweight tear-away stabilizer

Note: A 6-1/2" square ruler is very helpful for this project.

Yardages are for 44/45"-wide fabrics.

Cutting measurements include 1/4" seam allowances.

Cutting Instructions

From assorted bright print fat quarters, cut:
(25) 4" small block center squares.

From white print fabric, cut:
(1) 8" x 42" strip.
From the strip, cut:
(5) 8" appliqué block center squares.
(1) 3" x 13-1/2" appliqué block center rectangle.

From black fabric, cut:
(9) 3-1/2" x 42" strips.
From the strips, cut:
(10) 3-1/2" x 16" background rectangles,
(2) 3-1/2" x 14-1/2" background rectangles and
(12) 3-1/2" x 10" background rectangles.
(20) 2-1/2" x 42" strips.
From the strips, cut:
(50) 2-1/2" x 9" background rectangles and
(50) 2-1/2" x 5" background rectangles.
(5) 1-1/2" x 42" inner border strips.

From striped fabric, cut:
(12) 1" x 42" strips.
From the strips, cut:
(50) 1" x 4" small block inner border strips and
(50) 1" x 5" small block inner border strips.

From yellow print fabric, cut:
(5) 1-1/2" x 42" strips.
From the strips, cut:
(10) 1-1/2" x 10" appliqué block inner border strips and
(10) 1-1/2" x 8" appliqué block inner border strips.
(1) 1" x 42" strip.
From the strip, cut:
(2) 1" x 13-1/2" appliqué block inner border strips and
(2) 1" x 4" appliqué block inner border strips.

From black print fabric, cut:
(5) 3-1/2" x 42" outer border strips.

From backing fabric, cut:
(2) 32" x 51" backing rectangles.

From turquoise fabric, cut:
(6) 2-1/4" x 42" binding strips.

Assembling the Blocks

1. For each small square block, you will need a 4" bright print center square, (2) 1" x 4" and (2) 1" x 5" striped inner border strips, and (2) 2-1/2" x 5" and (2) 2-1/2" x 9" black background rectangles.

2. Sew the 4" striped inner border strips to the top and bottom edges of the center squares as shown. Press the seam allowances toward the inner border.

3. Sew the 5" striped inner border strips to the left and right edges of the center squares as shown. Press the seam allowances toward the inner border.

4. Sew the 2-1/2" x 5" black background rectangles to the top and bottom edges of the inner borders as shown. Press the seam allowances toward the background.

5. Sew the 2-1/2" x 9" background rectangles to the left and right edges of the inner border as shown. Press the seam allowances toward the background.

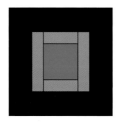

6. Use the 6-1/2" ruler to cut each small square block to 6-1/2" square, making sure the edges are at least 1/2" away from the corners of the striped inner border. Angle the ruler on the blocks, making 13 blocks that tilt to the right and 12 blocks that tilt to the left as shown.

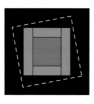

Make 13
tilted right *Make 12*
tilted left

7. Repeat Steps 1-5 to make the large square blocks, using an 8" white print center square, (2) 1-1/2" x 8" and (2) 1-1/2" x 10" yellow inner border strips, and (2) 3-1/2" x 10" and (2) 3-1/2" x 16" black background rectangles for each block. Cut each large square block to 12-1/2" square, making sure the edges are at least 1/2" away from the corners of the yellow inner border. Make 3 blocks that tilt to the right and 2 blocks that tilt to the left as shown.

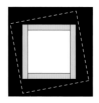 

Make 3
tilted right *Make 2*
tilted left

8. Repeat Steps 1-5 to make the rectangle block, using a 3" x 13-1/2" white print center rectangle, (2) 1" x 13-1/2" and (2) 1" x 4" yellow inner border strips, and (2) 3-1/2" x 14-1/2" and (2) 3-1/2" x 10" black background rectangles. Trim the rectangle block to measure 18-1/2" x 6-1/2", tilting this block to the right as shown.

Appliquéing the Blocks

1. Using the appliqué templates on pages 27 - 32, trace the shapes the number of times indicated for each block onto the paper side of the fusible web. For ease in identification, label each shape with the appropriate block number. Cut out the shapes, leaving a scant 1/4" around the outside of each shape.

2. Following the manufacturer's directions, fuse the web shapes on the wrong side of the assorted bright print fat quarters. Cut out each appliqué shape on the drawn line.

3. Sort the appliqué pieces for each block and remove the paper from the fusible web. Position the pieces onto each large square block and the rectangle block, referring to the block diagrams. Fuse the appliqué pieces on the blocks.

4. Cut a piece of tear-away stabilizer for each block slightly larger than the size of the fused appliqué pieces. Place the stabilizer on the back of the block, behind the appliqué. Stitch around each appliqué piece with a satin zigzag stitch or other programmed satin stitch. In addition, satin-stitch antennae on Blocks 1, 3, and 5. Carefully remove the stabilizer after stitching.

Assembling the Quilt Center

1. Lay out the appliquéd blocks and the small blocks on a large flat surface as shown in the diagram on page 26. Refer to this diagram for Steps 2-4.

2. Sew the small square blocks together in short horizontal rows or vertical columns. Press the seam allowances in one direction. Sew a row or column to each appliquéd block. Press the seam allowances toward the appliquéd blocks.

3. Sew the pieced units from Step 2 together to create three sections. Press the seam allowances in the direction needed to create the least bulk.

4. Sew the sections together to complete the quilt center. Press the seam allowances in one direction.

Section 1

Block 1

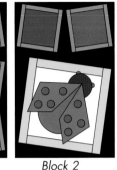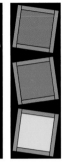

Block 2

Section 2

Block 3

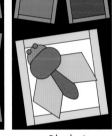

Block 4

Section 2

Block 5

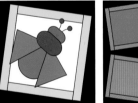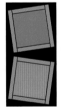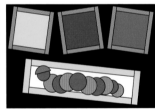

Block 6

Adding the Borders

1. Cut (2) 36-1/2" lengths from the 1-1/2"-wide black inner border strips. Sew these to the top and bottom edges of the quilt center. Press seam allowances toward the inner border.

2. Sew together the 3 remaining 1-1/2"-wide black inner border strips to make one long strip. From the strip, cut (2) 50-1/2" lengths. Sew these lengths to the left and right edges of the quilt center. Press the seam allowances toward the inner border.

3. Cut (2) 38-1/2" lengths from the 3-1/2"-wide black print outer border strips. Sew these to the top and bottom edges of the inner border. Press seam allowances toward the outer border.

4. Sew together the 3 remaining 3-1/2"-wide black print outer border strips to make one long strip. From the strip, cut (2) 56-1/2" lengths. Sew these lengths to the left and right edges of the inner border. Press the seam allowances toward the outer border.

Finishing the Quilt

1. Sew together the 32" x 51" backing rectangles along one long edge, using a 1/2" seam allowance. Press the seam allowances open.

2. Layer the pieced backing, the batting, and the quilt top. Baste the layers together and hand- or machine-quilt as desired.

3. Use diagonal seams to sew the 2-1/4"-wide black binding strips together to make one long strip. Sew binding to the edges of the quilt.

4. Trim the extra batting and backing even with the edges of the quilt top. Turn the binding over the edge to the back and hand- or machine-sew in place.

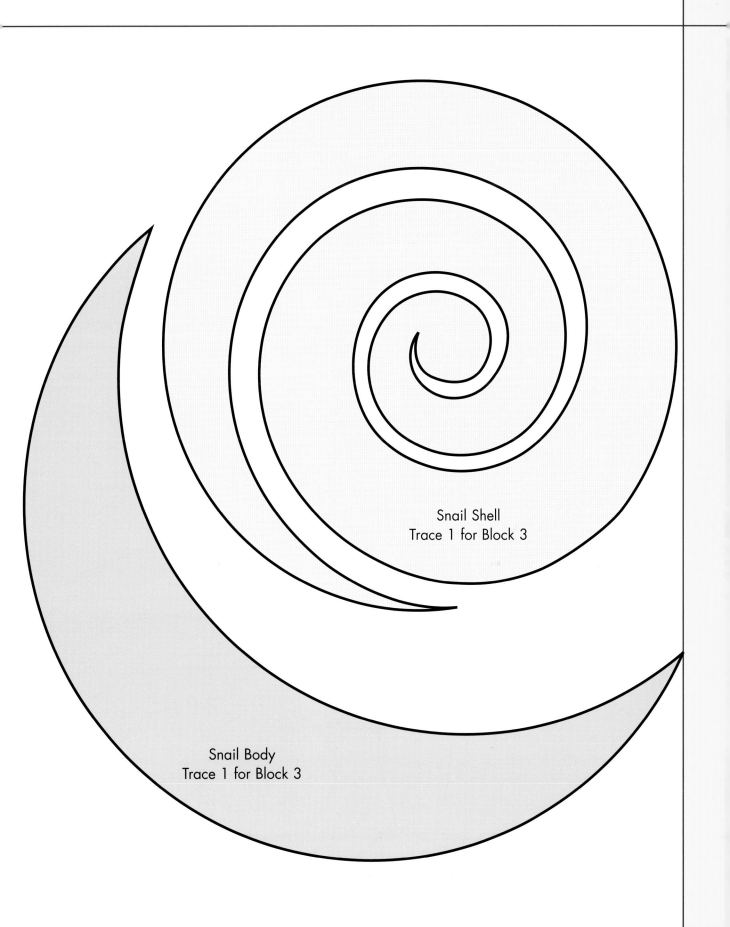

Snail Shell
Trace 1 for Block 3

Snail Body
Trace 1 for Block 3

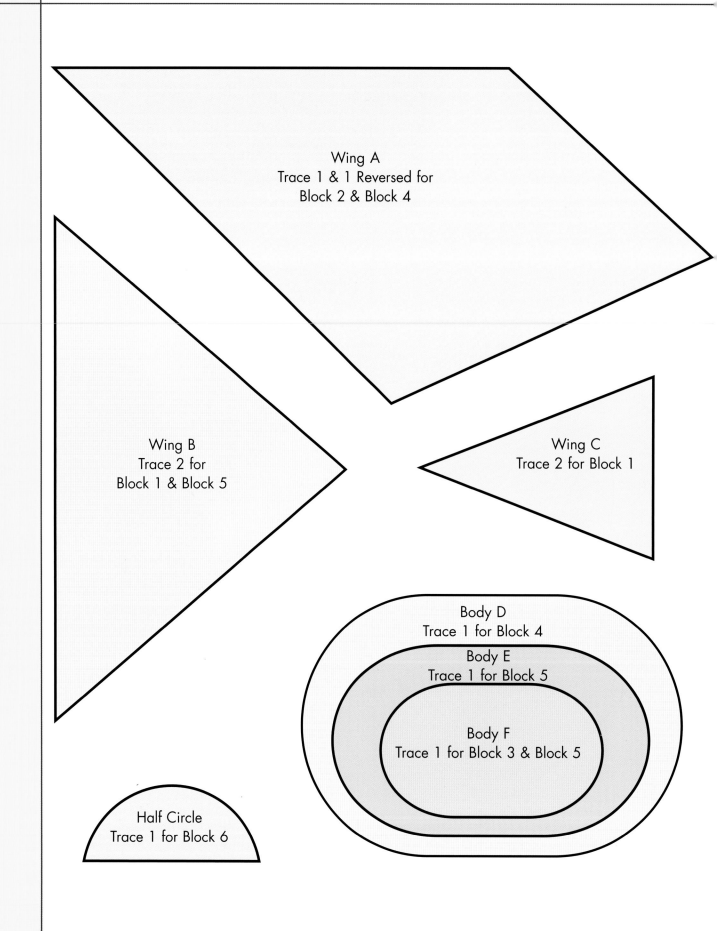

Wing A
Trace 1 & 1 Reversed for
Block 2 & Block 4

Wing B
Trace 2 for
Block 1 & Block 5

Wing C
Trace 2 for Block 1

Body D
Trace 1 for Block 4

Body E
Trace 1 for Block 5

Body F
Trace 1 for Block 3 & Block 5

Half Circle
Trace 1 for Block 6

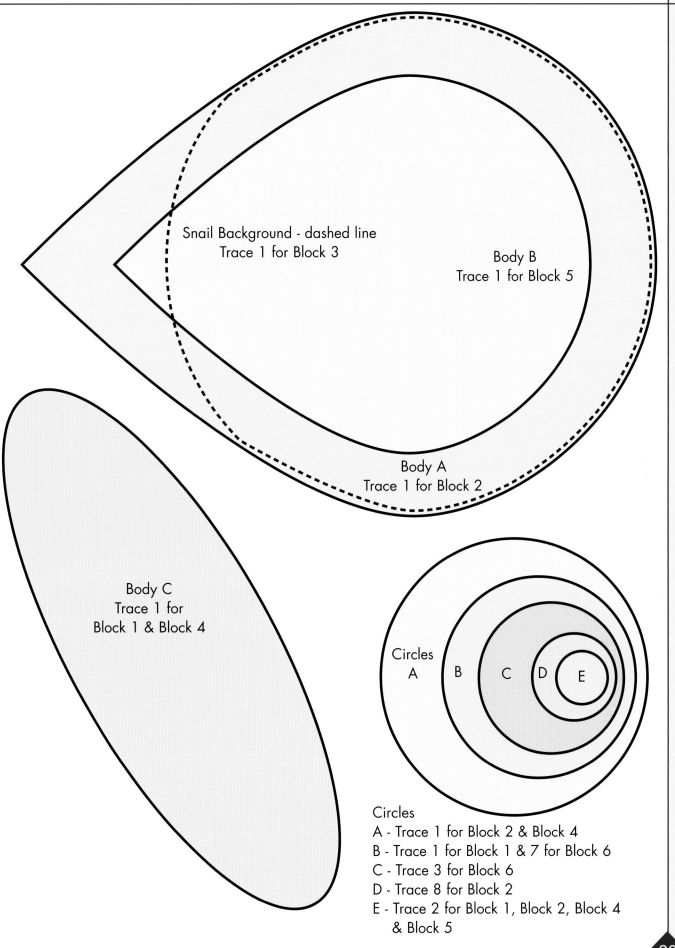

Snail Background - dashed line
Trace 1 for Block 3

Body B
Trace 1 for Block 5

Body A
Trace 1 for Block 2

Body C
Trace 1 for
Block 1 & Block 4

Circles
A   B   C   D   E

Circles
A - Trace 1 for Block 2 & Block 4
B - Trace 1 for Block 1 & 7 for Block 6
C - Trace 3 for Block 6
D - Trace 8 for Block 2
E - Trace 2 for Block 1, Block 2, Block 4
    & Block 5

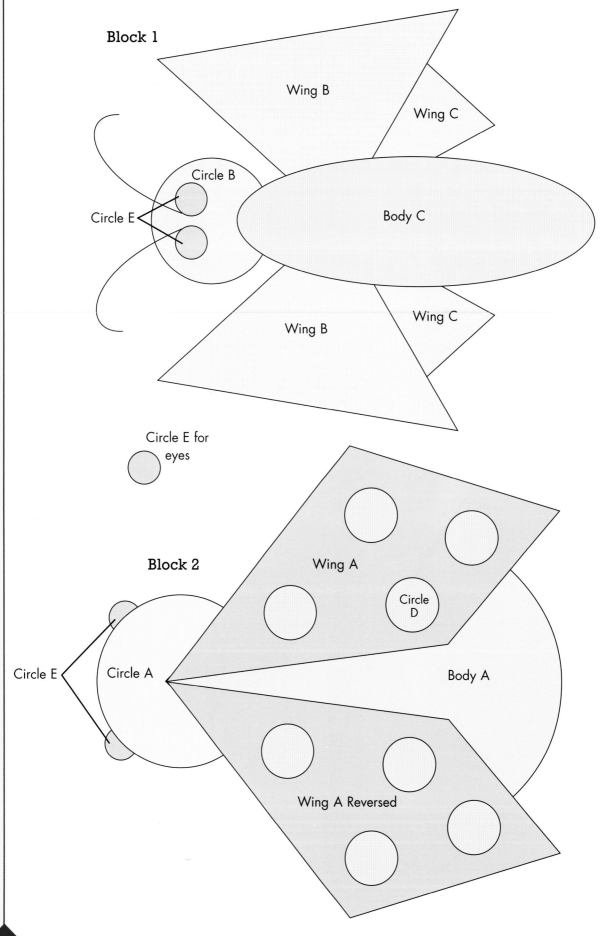

Block 1

Wing B

Wing C

Circle B

Circle E

Body C

Wing B

Wing C

Circle E for eyes

Block 2

Wing A

Circle
D

Circle E

Circle A

Body A

Wing A Reversed

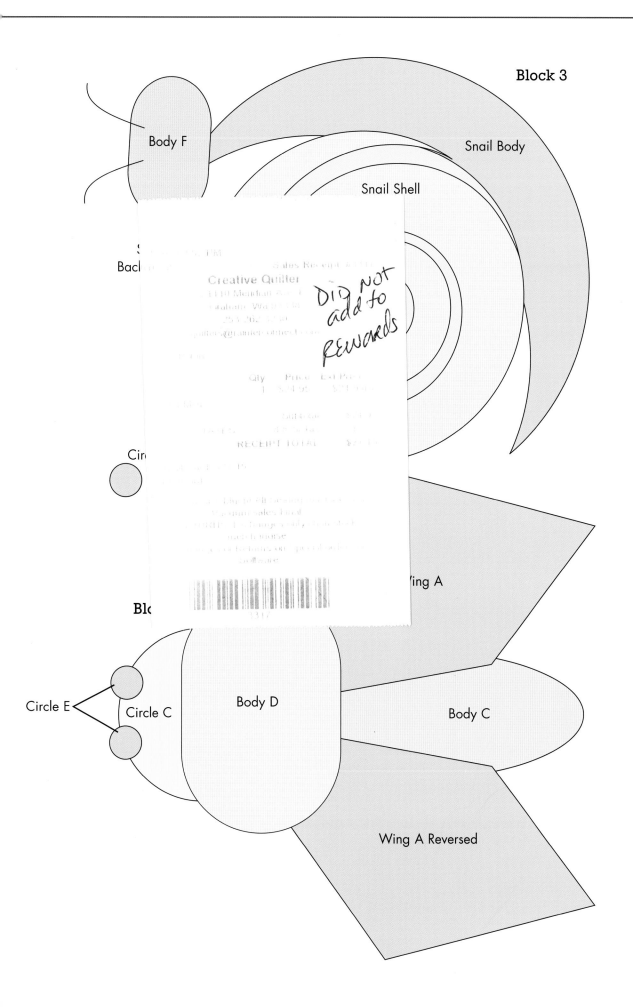

Block 3

Body F

Snail Body

Snail Shell

Back

Circle

Wing A

Block

Circle E

Circle C

Body D

Body C

Wing A Reversed

[Handwritten note on receipt:] DID NOT add to REWARDS

[Receipt text, partially legible:]

Creative Quilter

RECEIPT TOTAL

Block 5

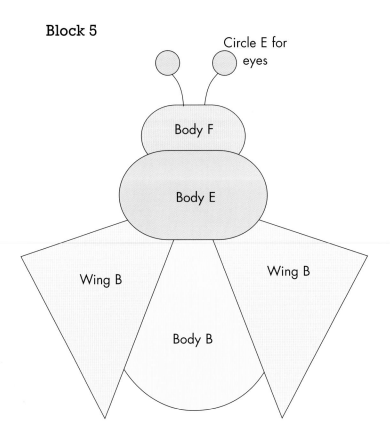

Circle E for eyes

Body F

Body E

Wing B

Wing B

Body B

Block 6

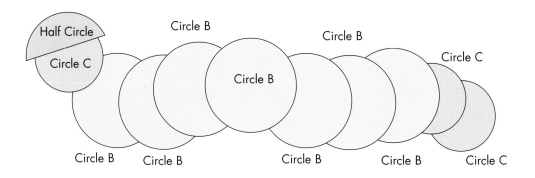

Half Circle

Circle C

Circle B

Circle B

Circle B

Circle C

Circle B

Circle B

Circle B

Circle B

Circle B

Circle C

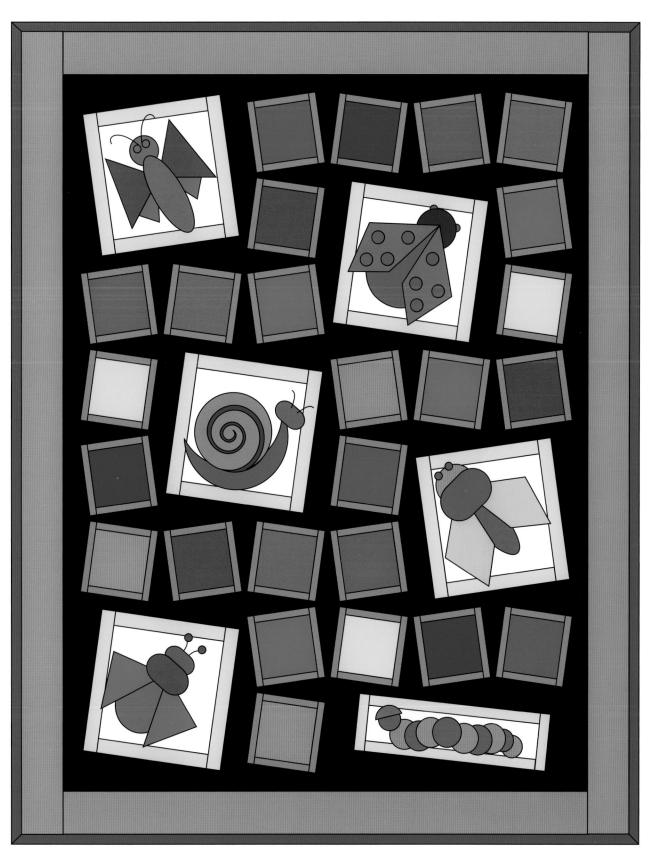

Buggy Nights Quilt

Treat that special little cowboy in your life to his own personalized western-theme nine-patch and appliqué wallhanging.

sheriff billy

Finished Size:
42-1/2" x 54-1/2"

Block Size:
6-1/2" square

Materials

1-1/8 yards of white fabric for 9-patch and appliqué blocks

5/8 yard of red print fabric for 9-patch blocks

1/3 yard of gold felted-wool fabric or wool felt for appliqués

1-5/8 yards of cowboy-motif fabric for border

2-3/4 yards of backing fabric

1/2 yard of black fabric for binding

Lightweight tear-away stabilizer

Fabric glue stick

Monofilament invisible thread

49" x 61" piece of batting

Optional: 102—1/2"-diameter black buttons and embroidery floss (buttons are a choking hazard so do not use if making project for a crib quilt)

Yardages are for 44/45"-wide fabrics.

Cutting measurements include 1/4" seam allowances.

Cutting Instructions

From white fabric, cut:
(7) 2-1/2" x 42" strips.
(3) 6-1/2" x 42" strips.
From the strips, cut:
(17) 6-1/2" block squares.

From red print fabric, cut:
(8) 2-1/2" x 42" strips.

From cowboy-motif fabric, cut:
(2) 6-1/2" x 42-1/2" side border strips.

Note: *Cut these strips parallel to the selvage edge of the fabric due to the directional pattern.*

(2) 6-1/2" x 30-1/2" top and bottom border strips.

From backing fabric, cut:
(2) 31" x 49" backing rectangles.

From black fabric, cut:
(6) 2-1/2" x 42" binding strips.

Assembling the 9-Patch Blocks

1. Sew together (1) 2-1/2"-wide white strip and (2) 2-1/2"-wide red print strips as shown to make one A strip set. Press seam allowances toward the red print strip. Repeat to make two additional strip sets. Cut each A strip set into 2-1/2"-wide segments as shown for a total of 44 A segments.

Make 3 A strip sets

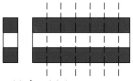

Make 44 A segments

2. Sew together (2) 2-1/2"-wide white strips and (1) 2-1/2"-wide red print strip as shown to make one B strip set. Press seam allowances toward the red print strip. Repeat to make a second B strip set. Cut 2-1/2"-wide segments from these strip sets for a total of 22 B segments.

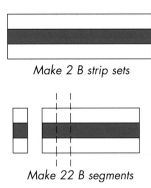

Make 2 B strip sets

Make 22 B segments

3. Sew together two A segments and one B segment to make a 9-Patch block as shown. Press the seam allowances toward the center segment. Check to be sure your block measures 6-1/2" square including seam allowances. Repeat to make 22 blocks.

Make 22 blocks

Appliquéing the Blocks

1. Personalize your wallhanging with embroidery if desired, using your sewing machine or a commercial embroidery shop. Place tear-away stabilizer on the back of the gold felted-wool fabric. Embroider "Sheriff" and the child's name 17 times on the fabric, spacing the embroidery to allow enough fabric around each for the badge shape. Each completed personalization should measure no more than 2" wide and 1" tall. Carefully remove the stabilizer after stitching. Use the template on page 38 to trace the badge shape 17 times onto the felted-wool fabric, centering an embroidered personalization within each badge shape.

2. Center a badge on each 6-1/2" white block square and tack in place with a fabric glue stick. Machine-appliqué along the edges of each badge using monofilament thread and a narrow zigzag stitch.

Assembling the Quilt Center

1. Lay out the appliquéd blocks and 18 of the 9-patch blocks on a large flat surface as shown in Wallhanging Center Assembly Diagram.

2. Sew the blocks together in seven horizontal rows, pressing the seam allowances toward the 9-patch blocks. Sew the rows together to complete the quilt center. Press the seam allowances in one direction.

Wallhanging Center
Assembly Diagram

Adding the Border

1. Sew the 6-1/2" x 42-1/2" cowboy-motif side border strips to the left and right edges of the wallhanging center. Press the seam allowances toward the border.

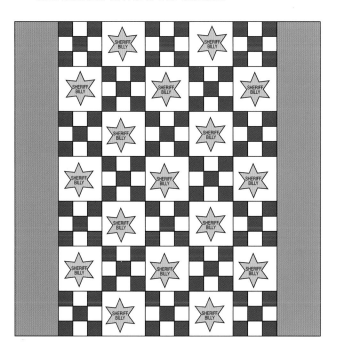

2. Sew a 9-patch block to each short edge of the 6-1/2" x 30-1/2" cowboy-motif top and bottom borders as shown. Press the seam allowances toward the border.

3. Sew the pieced borders from Step 2 to the top and bottom edges of the quilt center. Press the seam allowances toward the border.

Finishing the Wallhanging

1. Sew together the 31" x 46" backing rectangles along one long edge, using a 1/2" seam allowance. Press the seam allowances open.

2. Layer the pieced backing, the batting, and the wallhanging top. Baste the layers together and hand- or machine-quilt as desired.

3. Use diagonal seams to sew the 2-1/2"-wide black binding strips together to make one long strip. Sew binding to the edges of the wallhanging.

4. Trim the extra batting and backing even with the edges of the wallhanging top. Turn the binding over the edge to the back and hand- or machine-sew in place. Use black embroidery floss to sew a button to each point of all the badges. If project is going to be used as a crib quilt, do not add the buttons.

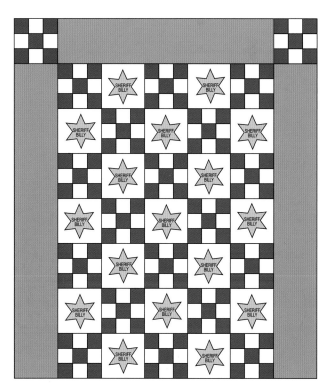

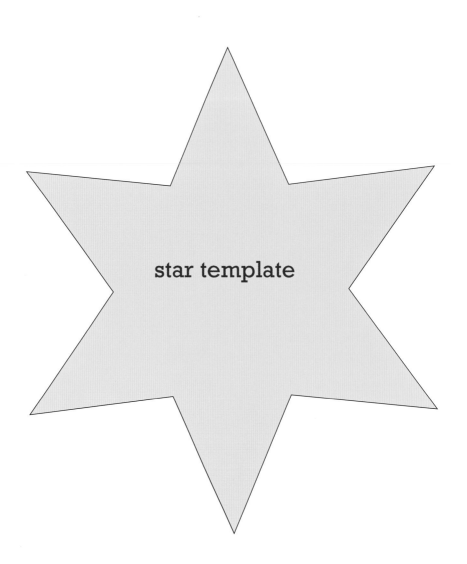

star template

Sheriff Billy Wallhanging

magic cape

Materials and **Yardage and cutting instructions** are for a child whose "B" measurement is 21" or less.

Materials

3/4 yard blue print fabric
for cape front

3/4 yard orange print fabric
for lining and appliqués

1/4 yard of light blue fabric
for star tail and appliqués

3/4 yard of contrasting blue print
fabric for binding

8" x 10" piece of blue dot fabric
for appliqués

1 yard of string

T-pin

Fabric marking pen

Lightweight paper-back fusible web

Lightweight tear-away stabilizer

Novelty threads for quilting

22" x 42" piece of lightweight
batting

2 squares of sew-on hook-and-loop
fastener

Cutting and Piecing Instructions

1. Measure circumference at the base of child's neck, add 1-1/2". Divide this measurement by 2. **This is measurement "A".**

2. Measure from collarbone to desired length of cape. Add the measurement of "A". **This is measurement "B".**

3. Fold the blue print fabric in half with right sides together, aligning the selvage edges. Tie one end of the string to the T-pin. Tie the string to the marking pen, keeping the length of measurement "A" between the T-pin and pen. Do not cut the excess string beyond the marking pen. Anchor the T-pin to the fold at one cut edge of the fabric. Draw a partial circle on the fabric with the marking pen by making an arc with the string as shown. This marks the neck opening.

4. Move the marking pen on the string, now keeping the length of measurement "B" between the T-pin and pen. Anchor the T-pin to the same point it was anchored when measurement "A" was marked. Again, draw a partial circle on the fabric with the marking pen by making an arc with the string. This will mark the bottom edge of the cape.

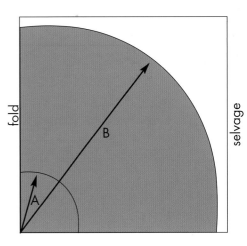

5. Cut through both layers of the fabric on the drawn lines for the cape front.

6. Using the orange print fabric, repeat steps 3-5 for cape lining. The remaining orange print fabric will be used for the star appliqués.

Adding the Appliqués

1. Using the appliqué templates on pages 42 - 43, trace the shapes the number of times indicated onto the paper side of the fusible web. Cut out the shapes, leaving a scant 1/4" around the outside of each shape.

2. Following the manufacturer's directions, fuse one small star web shape and two medium star shapes on the wrong side of the light blue fabric. Fuse the remaining small star shape and one medium star shape onto the wrong side of the orange print fabric. Fuse the final medium star shape and the star tail onto the wrong side of the blue dot fabric.

3. Cut out the star tail and the blue fabric stars on the drawn lines. Cut out the orange print stars and blue dot star a scant 1/4" inside the drawn lines, making them slightly smaller than the blue background stars they will be paired with. Remove the paper from the fusible web.

4. Position the star tail appliqué piece on the light blue star tail and fuse in place. Cut a piece of tear-away stabilizer slightly larger than the star tail. Place the stabilizer on the back of the tail. Stitch around the appliqué piece with a satin zigzag stitch. Carefully remove the stabilizer after stitching. Baste the open end of the appliquéd star tail to the cape front about 1-1/2" from the right-hand corner of the neck opening.

5. Refer to the photograph on page 40 to arrange the stars in pairs on the cape front, positioning the small pair over the basted end of the star tail. Fuse the stars in place. Cut a piece of stabilizer slightly larger than each layered star. Place the stabilizer on the wrong side of the cape front. Stitch around each appliqué piece with a satin zigzag stitch. Remove the stabilizer after stitching.

Finishing the Cape

1. Layer the lining, the batting, and the cape front. Baste the layers together. Machine-quilt to outline the appliquéd stars two or three times. Machine-quilt stars over the cape, using the small, medium, and large star templates.

2. Use diagonal seams to sew the 2-1/2"-wide blue print binding strips together to make one long strip. Sew the binding to the edges of the cape.

3. Trim the extra batting and lining even with the edges of the cape front. Turn the binding over the edge to the lining and hand- or machine-sew in place.

4. Hand-sew the loop side of the fasteners to the back of the star tail. Machine-sew the hook side of the fasteners on the opposite side of the cape, aligning them with those on the tail.

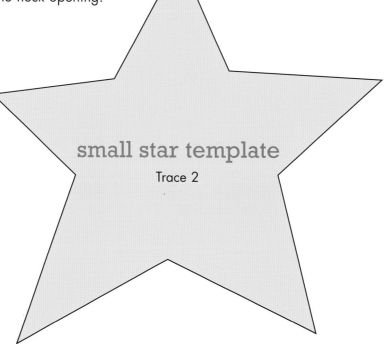

small star template

Trace 2

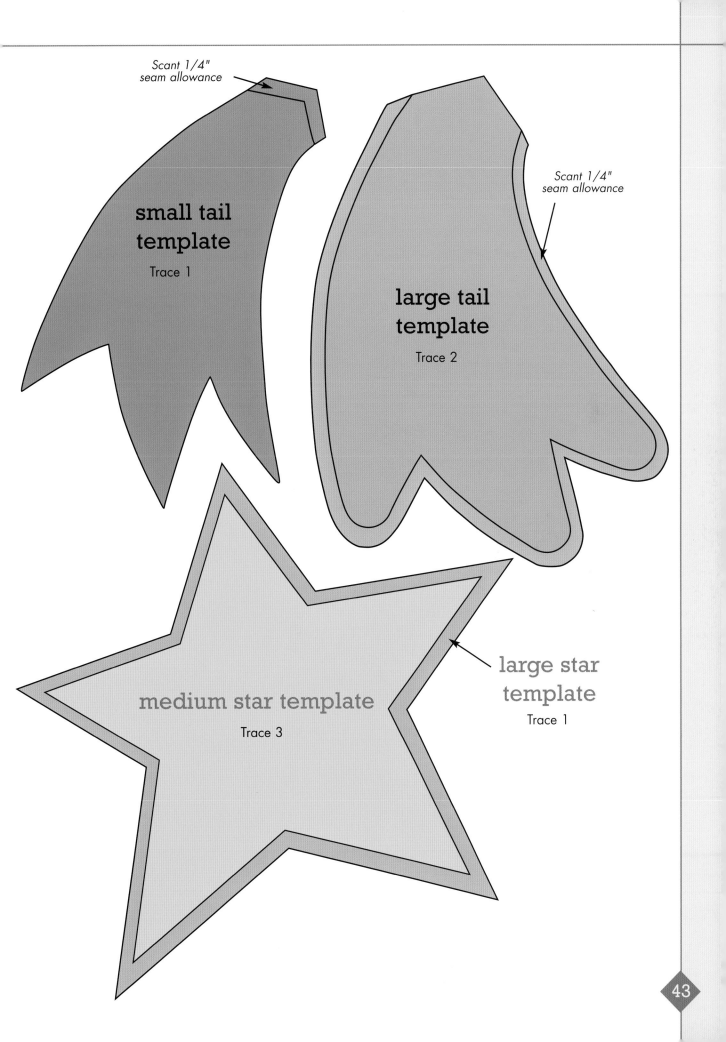

Scant 1/4"
seam allowance

small tail template

Trace 1

Scant 1/4"
seam allowance

large tail template

Trace 2

medium star template

Trace 3

large star template

Trace 1

43

Boys and girls alike will love toting this colorful variation on traditional plaid patchwork to the beach.

beach quilt

Finished Size:
33-1/2" x 47-1/2"

Materials

2/3 yard of dark blue print fabric for quilt center

1 yard of medium blue print fabric for quilt center and binding

1/4 yard of pale blue print for quilt center

1/4 yard of dark green fish-motif fabric for quilt center

1/2 yard of medium green print fabric for quilt center

1 yard of blue-green print fabric for quilt center and border

1-1/2 yards of backing fabric

40" x 54" piece of batting

Yardages are for 44/45"-wide fabrics.

Cutting measurements include 1/4" seam allowances.

Cutting Instructions

From dark blue print fabric, cut:
- (1) 3-1/2" x 42" A strip.
- (4) 2-1/2" x 42" A strips.
- (4) 1-1/2" x 42" A strips.

From medium blue print fabric, cut:
- (1) 3-1/2" x 42" strip.
  From the strip, cut:
  (1) 3-1/2" x 21" B strip.
- (5) 2-1/2" x 42" strips.
  From the strips, cut:
  (4) 2-1/2" x 21" B strips; reserve extra for 3 A strips.
- (5) 2-1/4" x 42" binding strips.
- (5) 1-1/2" x 42" strips.
  From the strips, cut:
  (4) 1-1/2" x 21" B strips; reserve extra for 3 A strips.

From pale blue print fabric, cut:
- (2) 2-1/2" x 42" strips.
  From the strips, cut:
  (3) 2-1/2" x 21" B strips.
- (2) 1-1/2" x 42" strips.
  From the strips, cut:
  (3) 1-1/2" x 21" B strips.

From dark green fish-motif fabric, cut:
- (1) 2-1/2" x 42" strip.
  From the strip, cut:
  (2) 2-1/2" x 21" C strips.
- (2) 1-1/2" x 42" strips.
  From the strips, cut:
  (3) 1-1/2" x 21" C strips.

From medium green print fabric, cut:
- (3) 2-1/2" x 42" strips.
  From the strips, cut:
  (2) 2-1/2" x 21" B strips.
  (3) 2-1/2" x 21" C strips.
- (3) 1-1/2" x 42" strips.
  From the strips, cut:
  (3) 1-1/2" x 21" B strips.
  (3) 1-1/2" x 21" C strips.

From blue-green print fabric, cut:
- (1) 3-1/2" x 42" strip.
  From the strip, cut:
  (1) 3-1/2" x 21" C strip.
- (4) 2-1/2" x 42" strips.
  From the strips, cut:
  (4) 2-1/2" x 21" C strips; reserve extra for 2 A strips.

(10) 1-1/2" x 42" strips.
   From the strips, cut:
   (4) 1-1/2" x 21" C strips.
   (2) 1-1/2" x 33-1/2" border strips; reserve
   extra for 3 A strips and 3 border strips.

From backing fabric, cut:
   (1) 40" x 54" backing rectangle.

Assembling the Strip Set Segments

1. For Strip Set A, arrange (1) 3-1/2" x 42"
    dark blue print strip, (4) 2-1/2" x 42" dark
    blue print strips, (4) 1-1/2" x 42" dark
    blue print strips, (3) 2-1/2" x 42" medium
    blue print strips, (3) 1-1/2" x 42" medium
    blue print strips, (2) 2-1/2" x 42" blue-green
    print strips, and (3) 1-1/2" x 42" blue-green
    print strips as shown. Sew the long edges of
    the strips together, pressing the seam
    allowances open.

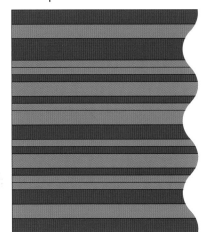

Strip Set A Assembly

2. From Strip Set A, cut (3) 3-1/2"-wide A
    segments, (4) 2-1/2"-wide A segments, and
    (4) 1-1/2"-wide A segments as shown.

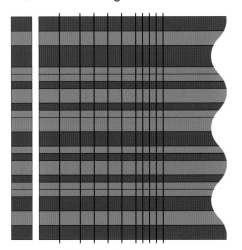

Strip Set A Cutting

3. For Strip Set B, arrange (1) 3-1/2" x 21"
    medium blue print strip, (4) 2-1/2" x 21"
    medium blue print strips, (4) 1-1/2" x 21"
    medium blue print strips, (3) 2-1/2" x 21"
    pale blue print strips, (3) 1-1/2" x 21" pale
    blue print strips, (2) 2-1/2" x 21" medium
    green print strips, and (3) 1-1/2" x 21"
    medium green print strips as shown. Sew the
    long edges of the strips together, pressing the
    seam allowances open.

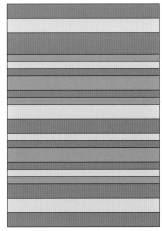

Strip Set B Assembly

4. From Strip Set B, cut (2) 2-1/2"-wide B
    segments and (7) 1-1/2"-wide B segments
    as shown.

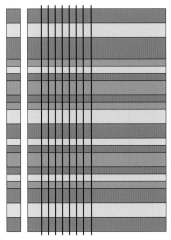

Strip Set B Cutting

5. For Strip Set C, arrange (1) 3-1/2" x 21" blue-green print strip, (4) 2-1/2" x 21" blue-green print strips, (4) 1-1/2" x 21" blue-green print strips, (2) 2-1/2" x 21" dark green fish-motif strips, (3) 1-1/2" x 21" dark green fish-motif strips, (3) 2-1/2" x 21" medium green print strips, and (3) 1-1/2" x 21" medium green print strips as shown. Sew the long edges of the strips together, pressing the seam allowances open.

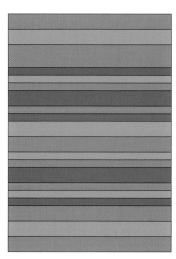

Strip Set C Assembly

6. From Strip Set C, cut (4) 2-1/2"-wide C segments and (5) 1-1/2"-wide C segments as shown.

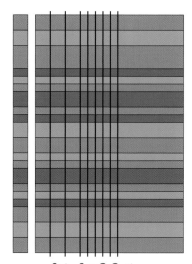

Strip Set C Cutting

Assembling the Quilt Center

1. Lay out the A, B, and C strip set segments on a large flat surface as shown.

2. Sew the segments together to complete the quilt center. Press the seam allowances in one direction.

Strip Set Layout

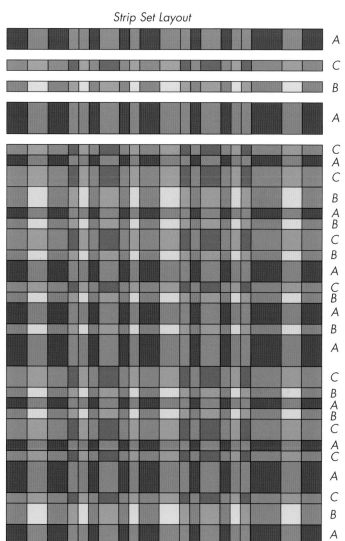

Adding the Borders

1. Sew together the (3) 1-1/2" x 42" blue-green print border strips to make one long strip. From the strip, cut (2) 1-1/2" x 45-1/2" side border strips. Sew these to the left and right edges of the quilt center. Press the seam allowances toward the border.

2. Sew the 1-1/2" x 33-1/2" border strips to the top and bottom edges of the quilt center. Press the seam allowances toward the border.

Finishing the Quilt

1. Layer the 40" x 54" backing rectangle, the batting, and the quilt top. Baste the layers together and hand- or machine-quilt as desired.

2. Use diagonal seams to sew the 2-1/4"-wide medium blue print binding strips together to make one long strip. Sew binding to the edges of the quilt.

3. Trim the extra batting and backing even with the edges of the quilt top. Turn the binding over the edge to the back and hand- or machine-sew in place.

Beach Quilt

TO DORM

Off to school—
Be sure to pack his
personal quilt.

Try the Bachelor's
Wheel or an easy
pieced creation in
school colors for your
athlete or musician.

Whether decorating the dorm room or tailgating on game day, this dramatic quilt is a perfect school companion.

bachelor's wheel

Finished Size:
74-1/2" x 98-1/2"

Block Size:
12" square

Materials
4-1/4 yards of black fabric for blocks, outer border, and binding

3 yards of shirting fabric for blocks

1-1/2 yards of red fabric for blocks and inner border

6 yards of backing fabric

80" x 104" piece of batting

Yardages are for 44/45"-wide fabrics.

Cutting measurements include 1/4" seam allowances.

Cutting Instructions
From black fabric, cut:
   (13) 3-7/8" x 42" strips.
      From the strips, cut:
      (129) 3-7/8" half-square triangle squares.
   (6) 3-1/2" x 42" strips.
      From the strips, cut:
      (70) 3-1/2" squares.
   (8) 6-1/2" x 42" outer border strips.
   (9) 2-1/4" x 42" binding strips.

From shirting fabric, cut:
   (14) 3-7/8" x 42" strips.
      From the strips, cut:
      (140) 3-7/8" half-square triangle squares.
   (12) 3-1/2" x 42" strips.
      From the strips, cut:
      (140) 3-1/2" squares.

From red fabric, cut:
   (9) 3-7/8" x 42" strips.
      From the strips, cut:
      (81) 3-7/8" half-square triangle squares.
   (8) 1-1/2" x 42" inner border strips.

From backing fabric, cut:
   (2) 40-1/2" x 104" backing rectangles.

Making the Half-Square Triangles
1. Draw a diagonal line on the wrong side of (140) 3-7/8" shirting squares.

2. With right sides together, layer the 3-7/8" shirting squares on (46) 3-7/8" red squares and (94) 3-7/8" black squares. Sew 1/4" from each side of the drawn lines.

3. Cut on the drawn line between the stitching. Press the seam allowances toward the red or black fabric. Check to be sure your 92 shirting/red and 188 shirting/black half-square triangles each measure 3-1/2" square; trim if necessary.

Make 92   *Make 188*

4. Repeat Steps 1-3 with (35) 3-7/8" red squares and (35) 3-7/8" black squares to make 70 red/black half-square triangles.

Make 70

Assembling the Blocks

1. For Block A, arrange 4 shirting/red half-square triangles, 4 shirting/black half-square triangles, 2 red/black half-square triangles, (2) 3-1/2" black squares, and (4) 3-1/2" shirting squares as shown. Sew the pieces together in rows, pressing the seam allowances in alternating directions from row to row. Sew the rows together to complete one block. Repeat to make a second A block.

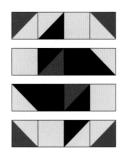 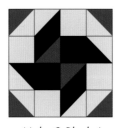

Make 2 Block A

2. For Block B, arrange 3 shirting/red half-square triangles, 5 shirting/black half-square triangles, 2 red/black half-square triangles, (2) 3-1/2" black squares, and (4) 3-1/2" shirting squares as shown. Sew the pieces together in rows, pressing the seam allowances in alternating directions from row to row. Sew the rows together to complete

one block. Repeat to make a total of 18 Block B.

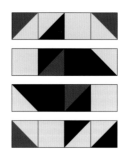 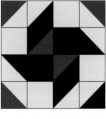

Make 18 Block B

3. For Block C, arrange 2 shirting/red half-square triangles, 6 shirting/black half-square triangles, 2 red/black half-square triangles, (2) 3-1/2" black squares, and (4) 3-1/2" shirting squares as shown. Sew the pieces together in rows, pressing the seam allowances in alternating directions from row to row. Sew the rows together to complete one block. Repeat to make a total of 15 Block C.

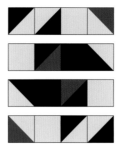 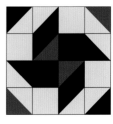

Make 15 Block C

Assembling the Quilt Center

1. Lay out the blocks on a large flat surface, taking care to position them in the direction shown on page 55 for the correct color placement. Place Block A at the top right and bottom left corners, Block B along the outer edges, and Block C in the center.

2. Sew the blocks together into rows. Press the seam allowances of each row to one side, alternating the direction with each row. Sew the rows together to complete the quilt center. Press the seam allowances in one direction.

Adding the Borders

1. Sew the 1-1/2"-wide red inner border strips together to make one long strip. From the strip, cut (2) 1-1/2" x 60-1/2" top and bottom inner border strips and (2) 1-1/2" x 86-1/2" side inner border strips.

2. Sew the 60-1/2" lengths to the top and bottom edges of the quilt center. Press the seam allowances toward the inner border. Sew the 86-1/2" lengths to the left and right edges of the quilt center. Press the seams toward the inner border.

3. Sew together the 6-1/2"-wide black border strips to make one long strip. From the strip, cut (2) 6-1/2" x 62-1/2" top and bottom outer border strips and (2) 6-1/2" x 98-1/2" side outer border strips.

4. Sew the 62-1/2" lengths to the top and bottom edges of the inner border. Press the seam allowances toward the outer border. Sew the 98-1/2" lengths to the left and right edges of the inner border. Press the seam allowances toward the outer border.

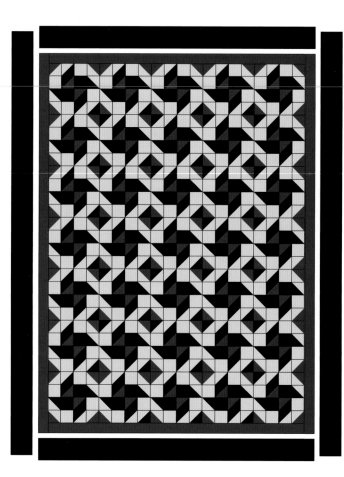

Finishing the Quilt

1. Sew together the 40-1/2" x 104" backing rectangles along one long edge, using a 1/2" seam allowance. Press the seam allowances open.

2. Layer the pieced backing, the batting, and the quilt top. Baste the layers together and hand- or machine-quilt as desired.

3. Use diagonal seams to sew the 2-1/4"-wide black binding strips together to make one long strip. Sew binding to the edges of the quilt.

4. Trim the extra batting and backing even with the edges of the quilt top. Turn the binding over the edge to the back and hand- or machine-sew in place.

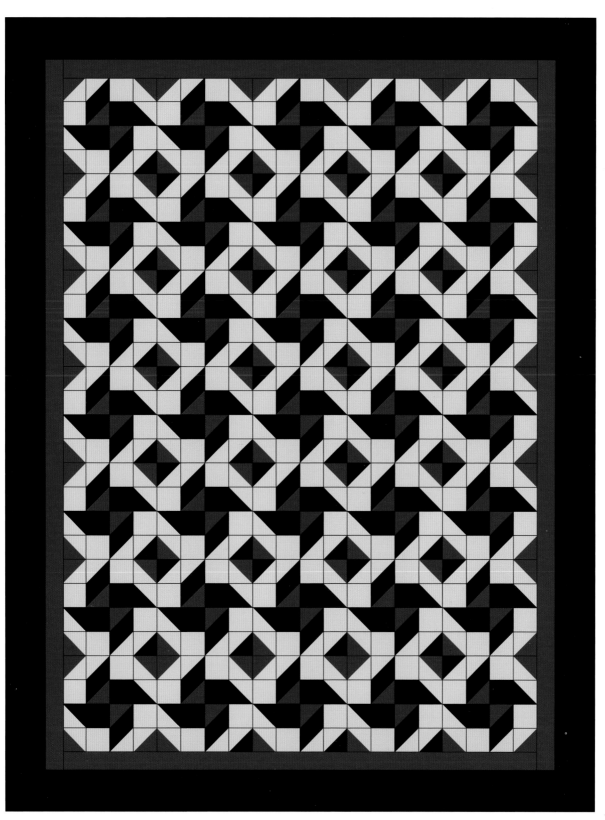

Bachelor's Wheel Quilt

huddle up

Finished Size:
64-1/2" x 76-1/2"

Block Size:
12" square

Materials

2 yards of green fabric for blocks, border, and binding

2 yards of black fabric for blocks and letter appliqués

1-1/2 yards of football-motif fabric for blocks

1 yard of orange fabric for blocks

1 yard of football player-motif fabric for blocks

1/4 yard of brown fabric for football appliqués

1/8 yard of cream fabric for football accent appliqués

4 yards of backing fabric

Lightweight paper-back fusible web

Lightweight tear-away stabilizer

71" x 83" piece of batting

Yardages are for 44/45"-wide fabrics.

Cutting measurements include 1/4" seam allowances.

Cutting Instructions

From green fabric, cut:
(5) 12-7/8" squares; cut the squares in half diagonally to make 10 Block C half-square triangles.
(8) 2-1/2" x 42" binding strips.
(7) 2-1/2" x 42" border strips.

From black fabric, cut:
(8) 3-1/2" x 42" strips.
From the strips, cut:
(48) 3-1/2" x 6-1/2" Block B rectangles.
(7) 1-3/4" x 42" strips.
From the strips, cut:
(16) 1-3/4" x 6-1/2" Block A rectangles.
(16) 1-3/4" x 9" Block A rectangles.

From football-motif fabric, cut:
(5) 12-7/8" squares; cut the squares in half diagonally to make 10 Block C half-square triangles.
(10) 2-1/4" x 42" strips.
From the strips, cut:
(16) 2-1/4" x 9" Block A rectangles.
(16) 2-1/4" x 12-1/2" Block A rectangles.

From orange fabric, cut:
(2) 6-1/2" x 42" strips.
From the strips, cut:
(12) 6-1/2" Block B center squares.
(4) 3-1/2" x 42" strips.
From the strips, cut:
(48) 3-1/2" Block B corner squares.

From football player-motif fabric, fussy-cut:
(8) 6-1/2" Block A center squares, centering a football player in each square.

From backing fabric, cut:
(2) 42" x 71" backing rectangles.

Assembling the Blocks

1. For Block A, arrange (1) 6-1/2" football player-motif center square, (2) 1-3/4" x 6-1/2" black rectangles, (2) 1-3/4" x 9" black rectangles, (2) 2-1/4" x 9" football-motif rectangles, and (2) 2-1/4" x 12-1/2" football-motif rectangles as shown.

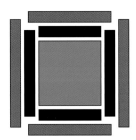

2. Sew the 1-3/4" x 6-1/2" black rectangles to the top and bottom edges of the center square as shown. Press the seam allowances toward the rectangles. Join the 1-3/4" x 9" black rectangles to the left and right edges of the center square; press the seam allowances toward the rectangles.

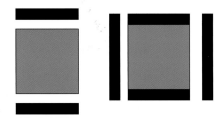

3. Sew the 2-1/4" x 9" football-motif rectangles to the top and bottom edges of black rectangles as shown; press the seam allowances away from the center. Join the 2-1/4" x 12-1/2" football-motif rectangles to the left and right edges of the black rectangles to complete one block. Press the seam allowances away from the center. Repeat Steps 1-3 to make 8 A blocks.

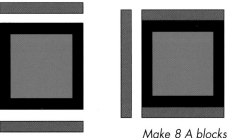

Make 8 A blocks

4. For Block B, arrange (1) 6-1/2" orange center square, (4) 3-1/2" orange corner squares, and (4) 3-1/2" x 6-1/2" black rectangles as shown. Sew the pieces together in rows, pressing the seam allowances toward the black rectangles. Sew the rows together to complete one block. Repeat to make 12 B blocks.

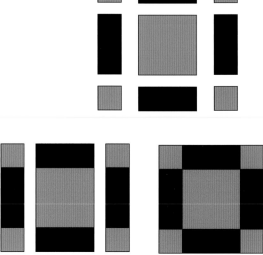

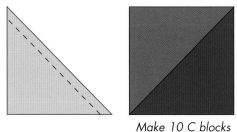

Make 12 B blocks

5. For Block C, sew together the long edges of a football-motif half-square triangle and a green half-square triangle. Press the seam allowances toward the green triangle. Repeat to make 10 C blocks.

Make 10 C blocks

Assembling the Quilt Center

1. Lay out the A, B, and C blocks on a large flat surface, taking care to position the C blocks in the direction shown for the correct color placement.

2. Sew the blocks together into rows. Press the seam allowances of each row to one side, alternating the direction with each row. Sew the rows together to complete the quilt

center. Press the seam allowances in one direction.

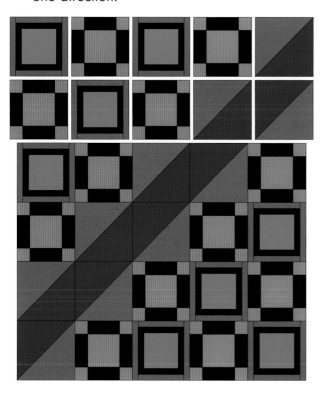

Adding the Border

1. Sew the 2-1/2"-wide green border strips together to make one long strip. From the strip, cut (2) 2-1/2" x 60-1/2" top and bottom border strips and (2) 2-1/2" x 76-1/2" side border strips.

2. Sew the 60-1/2" lengths to the top and bottom edges of the quilt center. Press the seam allowances toward the border. Sew the 76-1/2" lengths to the left and right edges of the quilt center. Press the seams toward the border.

Adding the Appliqués

1. Using the appliqué templates on pages 62 - 67, trace the letters needed to personalize your quilt and each football and football accent shape six times onto the paper side of the fusible web. Cut out the shapes, leaving a scant 1/4" around the outside of each shape.

2. Following the manufacturer's directions, fuse the letter shapes on the wrong side of the black fabric. Fuse the football shapes onto the wrong side of the brown fabric and the football accent shapes onto the wrong side of the cream fabric. Cut out each appliqué shape on the drawn line.

3. Refer to the diagram on page 69 to arrange the shapes on the quilt top and fuse in place. Cut a piece of tear-away stabilizer slightly larger than the size of the fused appliqué pieces. Place the stabilizer on the wrong side of the quilt top, behind the appliqué. Stitch around each appliqué piece with a narrow zigzag stitch. Carefully remove the stabilizer after stitching.

Finishing the Quilt

1. Sew together the 42" x 71" backing rectangles along one long edge, using a 1/2" seam allowance. Press the seam allowances open.

2. Layer the pieced backing, the batting, and the quilt top. Baste the layers together and hand- or machine-quilt as desired.

3. Use diagonal seams to sew the 2-1/2"-wide green binding strips together to make one long strip. Sew binding to the edges of the quilt.

4. Trim the extra batting and backing even with the edges of the quilt top. Turn the binding over the edge to the back and hand- or machine-sew in place.

Music Block Option

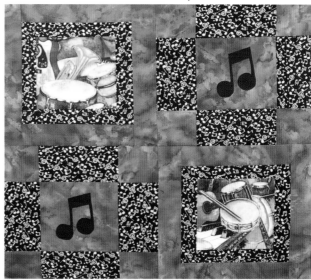

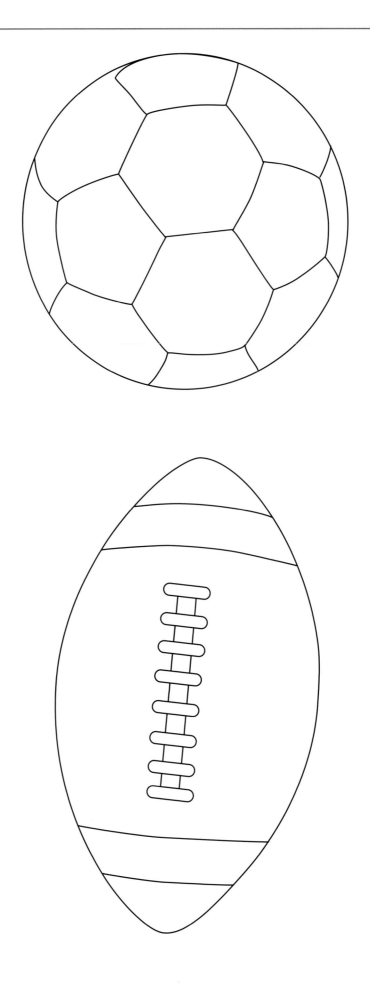

A B C

D E F

G H I

J K L M

N O P
Q R S T
U V W
X Y Z

A B C
D E F
G H I
J K L M

N O P

Q R S T

U V W

X Y Z

And The Band Played On Quilt

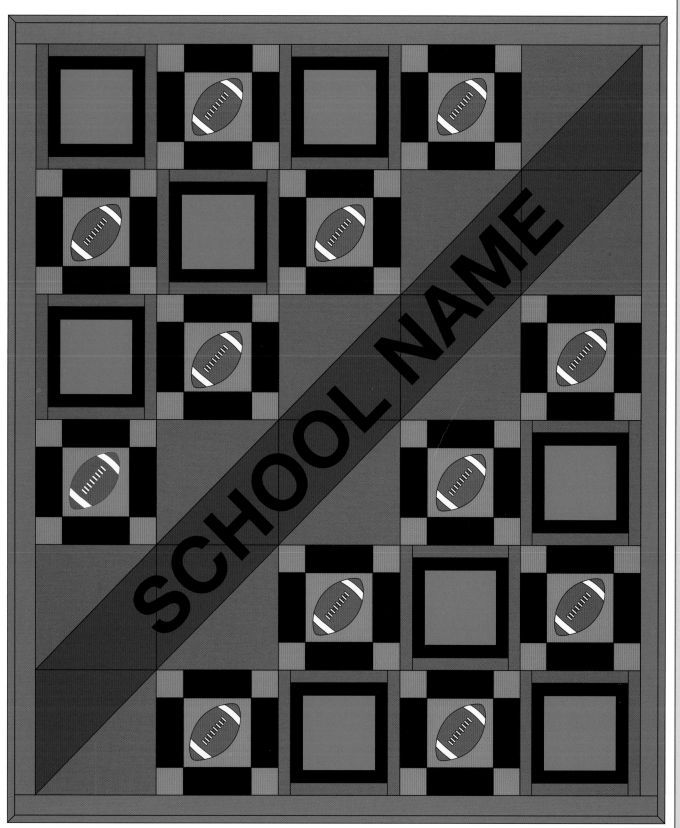

Huddle Up Quilt

TO DEN

There's no place like home for the warmth and welcome of a lap quilt recognizing his favorite pastimes.

Be inspired to create a quilted throw just for him.

patriot games

Finished Size:
50-1/2" x 50-1/2"

Materials

1-1/2 yards of cream fabric for blocks

1-1/2 yards of blue fabric for blocks

1-1/8 yards of copper fabric for blocks and outer border

1-5/8 yards of red fabric for blocks, inner border, and binding

3-1/4 yards of backing fabric

57" x 57" piece of batting

Yardages are for 44/45"-wide fabrics.

Cutting measurements include 1/4" seam allowances.

Cutting Instructions

From cream fabric, cut:
- (3) 4-1/2" x 42" 4-Patch block strips.
- (4) 2-1/8" x 42" Star block strips.
- (2) 4-7/8" x 42" strips.
  From the strips, cut:
  (15) 4/78" half-square triangle squares.
- (1) 4-1/2" x 42" strip.
  From the strip, cut:
  (2) 4-1/2" 4-Patch block squares.
- (4) 2" x 42" strips.
  From the strips, cut:
  (64) 2" Star block squares.

From blue fabric, cut:
- (4) 2-1/8" x 42" Star block strips.
- (3) 4-7/8" 42" strips.
  From the strips, cut:
  (18) 4-7/8" half-square triangle squares.
- (4) 2-1/2" x 42" strips.
  From the strips, cut: (64) 2-1/2" Star block squares.
- (8) 2" x 42" strips.
  From the strips, cut: (144) 2" Star block squares.

From copper fabric, cut:
- (3) 4-1/2" x 42" 4-Patch block strips.
- (1) 4-7/8" x 42" strip.
  From the strip, cut: (3) 4-7/8" half-square triangle squares.
- (2) 4-1/2" x 42" strips.
  From the strips, cut:
  (4) 4-1/2" x 14-1/2" outer border strips.
  (2) 4-1/2" 4-Patch block squares.
- (3) 2-1/2" x 42" strips.
  From the strips, cut: (40) 2-1/2" Star block squares.

From red fabric, cut:
- (4) 1-1/4" x 42" Star block strips.
- (7) 2-1/2" x 42" strips.
  From the strips cut: (104) 2-1/2" Star block squares.
- (5) 1-1/2" x 42" inner border strips. **Note:** *If your fabric is at least 42-1/2" wide, you will only need 4 strips.*
  Enough 2-1/4"-wide bias strips to total 220".

From backing fabric, cut:
- (2) 29" x 57" backing rectangles.

Making the Half-Square Triangles

1. Draw a diagonal line on the wrong side of (15) 4-7/8" cream squares and (3) 4-7/8" copper squares as shown.

2. With right sides together, layer the 4-7/8" cream and copper squares on (18) 4-7/8" blue squares. Sew 1/4" on each side of the drawn lines as shown.

3. Cut on the drawn line between the stitching as shown. Press the seam allowances toward the blue fabric. Check to be sure your 30 cream/blue and 6 copper/blue half-square triangles each measure 4-1/2" square. Trim if necessary.

Make 30   *Make 6*

Assembling the 4-Patch Blocks

1. Sew together one 4-1/2" x 42" cream strip and one 4-1/2" x 42" copper strip as shown to make one A strip set. Press seam allowances toward the copper strip. Repeat to make two additional strip sets. Cut 4-1/2"-wide segments from each A strip set as shown for a total of 20 A segments.

Make 3 A strip sets

4-1/2"
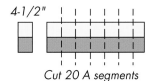

Cut 20 A segments

2. Sew together two A segments to make a 4-Patch A block as shown. Press the seam allowances in one direction. Check to be sure your block measures 8-1/2" square including seam allowances. Repeat to make a total of 8 4-Patch A blocks.

Make 8 A Blocks

3. For a 4-Patch B block, you will need a copper/blue half-square triangle, a 4-1/2" cream square and an A segment. Sew the pieces together as shown, pressing the first seam allowances toward the half-square triangle and the second seam allowances toward the A segment. Make 2 B blocks.

Make 2 B Blocks

4. For a 4-Patch C block, you will need a cream/blue half-square triangle, a 4-1/2" copper square and an A segment. Sew the pieces together as shown, pressing the first seam allowances toward the 4-1/2" square and the second seam allowances toward the A segment. Make 2 C blocks.

Make 2 C Blocks

Assembling the Star Blocks

1. Sew together (1) 1-1/4" x 42" red strip and (2) 2-1/8" x 42" cream strips as shown to make one B strip set. Press seam allowances toward the red strip. Repeat to make one additional strip set. Cut each B strip set into 2-1/2"-wide segments as shown for a total of 32 B segments.

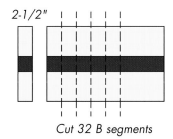

Make 2 B strip sets

Cut 32 B segments

2. Sew together (1) 1-1/4" x 42" red strip and (2) 2-1/8" x 42" blue strips as shown to make one C strip set. Press seam allowances toward the red strip. Repeat to make one additional strip set. Cut each C strip set into 2-1/2"-wide segments as shown for a total of 20 C segments.

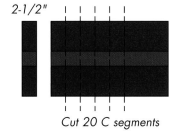

Make 2 C strip sets

Cut 20 C segments

3. Draw a diagonal line on the wrong side of (64) 2-1/2" blue squares and (40) 2-1/2" copper squares as shown.

4. With right sides together, align a 2-1/2" blue square with one end of a B segment as shown. Sew on the drawn line and trim the seam allowances to 1/4". Press open the attached triangle.

5. Sew another 2-1/2" blue square to the opposite end of the B segment in the same manner. Trim and press as before to make one Flying Geese unit as shown. Check to be sure the unit measures 2-1/2" x 4-1/2" including seam allowances. Repeat to make a total of 32 blue/cream Flying Geese units.

Make 32 Blue/Cream Units

6. Repeat Steps 4 and 5 with the 2-1/2" copper squares and the C segments to make 20 copper/blue Flying Geese units.

Make 20 Copper/Blue Units

7. Draw a diagonal line on the wrong side of (64) 2" cream squares and (144) 2" blue squares as shown.

8. With right sides together, align a 2" cream square with one corner of a 2-1/2" red square as shown. Sew on the drawn line and trim the seam allowances to 1/4". Press open the attached triangle.

9. Sew another 2" cream square to the opposite corner of the 2-1/2" red square. Trim and press as before to make one 3-piece square as shown. Check to be sure the square measures 2-1/2" including seam allowances. Repeat to make a total of 32 cream/red 3-piece squares.

Make 32 Cream/Red 3-piece Squares

10. Repeat Steps 8 and 9 with the 2" blue squares and the remaining 2-1/2" red squares to make 72 blue/red 3-piece squares.

Make 72 Blue/Red 3-piece Squares

11. Arrange 4 blue/red 3-piece squares as shown. Sew the squares together in pairs; press the seam allowances in opposite directions. Sew the pairs together to make one block center. Press the seam allowances in one direction.

Make 13 Star block centers

12. For a Star A block, you will need a block center, 4 blue/cream Flying Geese units, and 4 cream/red 3-piece squares. Sew the pieces together in rows, pressing the seam allowances away from the Flying Geese units. Sew the rows together to complete one Star A block. Repeat to make a total of 8 Star A blocks.

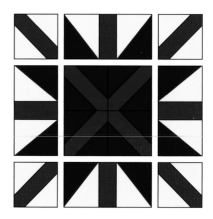

Make 8 Star A blocks

13. For a Star B block, you will need a block center, 4 copper/blue Flying Geese units, and 4 blue/red 3-piece squares. Sew the pieces together in rows, pressing the seam allowances away from the Flying Geese

units. Sew the rows together to complete one Star B block. Repeat to make a total of 5 Star B blocks.

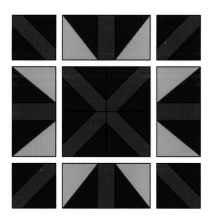

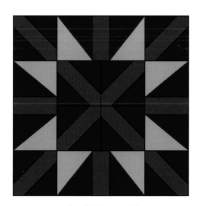

Make 5 Star B blocks

Assembling the Quilt Center

1. Lay out the 4-Patch A, 4-Patch B, 4-Patch C, Star A, and Star B blocks on a large flat surface as shown in the diagram.

2. Sew the block together into rows, pressing the seam allowances toward the 4-Patch blocks. Sew the rows together to complete the quilt center. Press the seam allowances in one direction.

Adding the Borders

1. Cut (2) 40-1/2" lengths from the 1-1/2"-wide red inner border strips. Sew these to the side edges of the quilt center. Press seam allowances toward the inner border.

2. Sew together the 3 remaining 1-1/2"-wide red inner border strips to make one long strip. From the strip, cut (2) 42-1/2" lengths. Sew these lengths to the top and bottom edges of the quilt center. Press seam allowances toward the inner border.

3. For each side outer border, sew together a 4-1/2" x 14-1/2" copper outer border strip and 7 cream/blue half-square triangles as shown. Press the seam allowances toward the copper strip. Sew these pieced borders to the left and right edges of the inner border, referring to the diagram on page 79 for the border direction. Press the seam allowances toward the inner border.

4. For each top and bottom outer border, sew together a 4-1/2" x 14-1/2" copper outer border strip, 7 cream/blue half-square triangles, and two copper/blue half-square triangles as shown. Press the seam allowances toward the copper strip. Sew these pieced borders to the top and bottom edges of the inner border, referring to the diagram on page 79 for the border direction. Press the seam allowances toward the inner border.

Top and Bottom Borders

Outer Side Borders

Finishing the Quilt

1. Sew together the 29" x 57" backing rectangles along one long edge, using a 1/2" seam allowance. Press the seam allowances open.

2. Layer the pieced backing, the batting, and the quilt top. Baste the layers together and hand- or machine-quilt as desired.

3. Use diagonal seams to sew the 2-1/4"-wide red binding strips together to make one long strip. Sew binding to the edges of the quilt.

4. Trim the extra batting and backing even with the edges of the quilt top. Turn the binding over the edge to the back and hand- or machine-sew in place.

Patriot Games Quilt

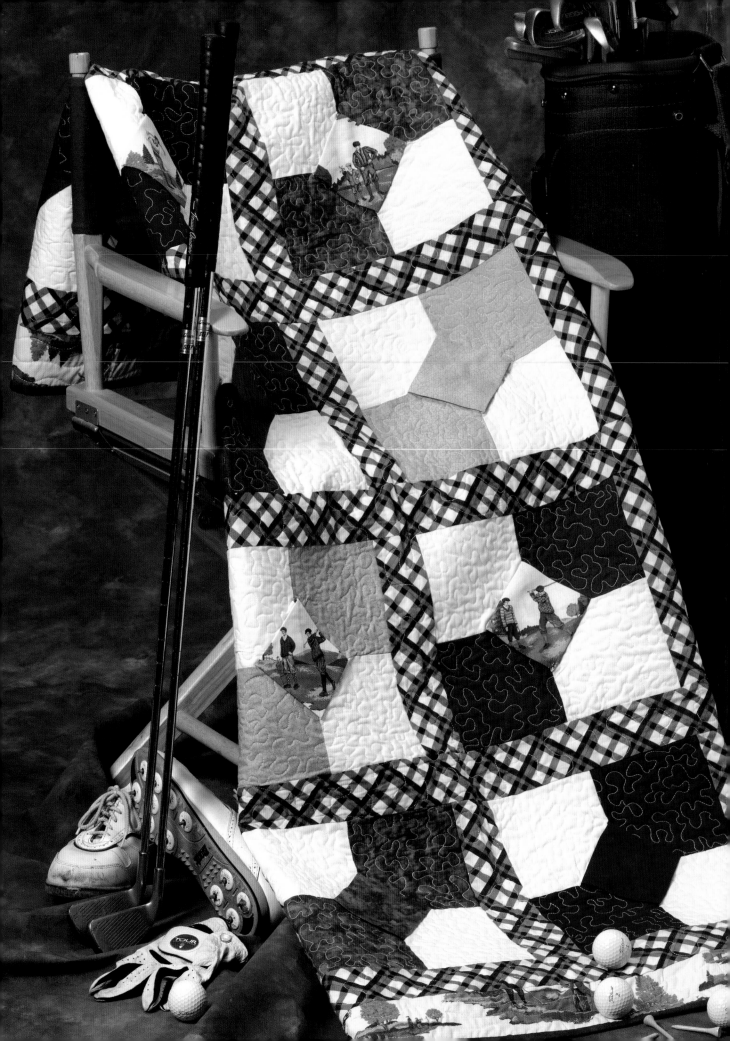

tee time

Finished Size:
58-1/2" x 71"

Block Size:
10" square

Materials
1 yard cream fabric for blocks

1/2 yard each of five dark fabrics for blocks

1-1/4 yards of plaid fabric for sashing

2 yards of golf-motif fabric for block centers and border

1/2 yard of burgundy fabric for binding

4-1/4 yards of backing fabric

65" x 77" piece of batting

Yardages are for 42"-wide fabrics.

Cutting measurements include 1/4" seam allowances.

Cutting Instructions

From cream fabric, cut:
(6) 5-1/2" x 42" strips.
From the strips, cut:
(40) 5-1/2" squares.

From each of the dark fabrics, cut:
(2) 5-1/2" x 42" strips.
From the strips, cut:
(8) 5-1/2" squares.
(2) 4-1/4" center squares.

From plaid fabric, cut:
(14) 3" x 42" strips.
From the strips, cut:
(15) 3" x 10-1/2" sashing strips.

From golf-motif fabric, cut:
(2) 3-1/4" x 71" side outer border strips
Note: *Cut these strips first, parallel to the selvage edge of the fabric, because of the directional pattern.*
Enough 3-1/4"-wide strips from the remaining width of the fabric to total 110" for the top and bottom outer border strips.
(10) 4-1/4" center squares, centering a golf-motif in each square.

From burgundy fabric, cut:
(7) 2-1/2" x 42" binding strips.

Assembling the Blocks
1. Arrange four 5-1/2" squares as shown, using two cream and two dark squares of the same color.

2. Sew the squares together into rows; press the seam allowances in opposite directions. Sew the rows together to complete the block. Press the seam allowances in one direction.

3. Taking a 4-1/4" center square of the same dark color, turn the edges under 1/4" on all sides. Press.

4. Position the 4-1/4" center square on the four-patch unit. Hand- or machine-appliqué in place.

5. Repeat Steps 1 to 4 to make a total of 20 blocks. Referring to page 83, use a golf-motif center square with two blocks of each dark color and use the same color fabric square with the remaining blocks.

Assembling the Quilt Center

1. Sew together the ten remaining 3" x 42" plaid strips to make one long strip. From this strip, cut (4) 3" x 48" sashing strips. Set aside the remaining plaid strip for the inner border.

2. Lay out the blocks, the 3" x 10-1/2" sashing strips, and the 3" x 48" sashing strips on a large flat surface as shown.

3. Sew the blocks and 3" x 10-1/2" sashing strips together into rows, pressing the seam allowances toward the sashing strips. Sew the rows together with the 3" x 48" sashing strips. Press the seam allowances toward the sashing strips.

Adding the Borders

1. From the set aside plaid strip, cut (2) 3" x 48" top and bottom inner border strips and (2) 3" x 65-1/2" side inner border strips.

2. Sew the 48" lengths to the top and bottom edges of the quilt center. Press seams toward the border. Sew the 65-1/2" lengths to the left and right edges of the quilt center. Press seams toward the border.

3. Sew together the 3-1/4"-wide golf-motif strips for the top and bottom outer border to make one long strip. From the strip, cut (2) 53" lengths and sew these lengths to the inner top and bottom border. Press the seam allowances toward the outer border.

4. Sew the 3-1/4" x 71" outer border strips to the left and right edges of the inner border. Press seams toward the outer border.

Finishing the Quilt

Layer the backing fabric, the batting, and the quilt top. Baste the layers together and hand- or machine-quilt as desired.

2. Use diagonal seams to sew the 2-1/2"-wide binding strips together to make one long strip. Sew binding to the edges of the quilt.

3. Trim the extra batting and backing, leaving 1/4" to 3/8" beyond the quilt top. Turn the binding over the edge to the back and hand- or machine-sew in place.

Tee Time Quilt

Any avid fisherman would love to catch this multi-hued gem set to Mother Nature's serene color palette.

fields & streams

Finished Size:
51-1/2" x 68-1/2"

Block Size:
12" square

Materials
20 or more assorted light print fat quarters for blocks

25 or more assorted dark print fat eighths for blocks

1/2 yard of dark green print fabric for binding

3-1/4 yards of backing fabric

58" x 75" piece of batting

Yardages are for 44/45"-wide fabrics.

Cutting measurements include 1/4" seam allowances.

Cutting Instructions
From light print fat quarters, cut a total of:
   (24) 9-1/4" squares; cut the squares into quarters diagonally to make 96 quarter-square A triangles.
   (43) 5-1/4" squares; cut the squares into quarters diagonally to make 172 quarter-square B triangles.
   (17) 4-7/8" squares; cut the squares in half diagonally to make 34 half-square C triangles.

From dark print fat quarters, cut a total of:
   (36) 5-1/4" squares; cut the squares into quarters diagonally to make 144 quarter-square B triangles.
   (24) 4-7/8" squares; cut the squares in half diagonally to make 48 half-square C triangles.

From dark green fabric, cut:
   (6) 2-1/2" x 42" binding strips.

From backing fabric, cut:
   (2) 38" x 58" backing rectangles.

Assembling the Blocks
1. For Block A, arrange 4 light print A triangles, 4 light print B triangles, 8 dark print B triangles, and 4 light print C triangles as shown.

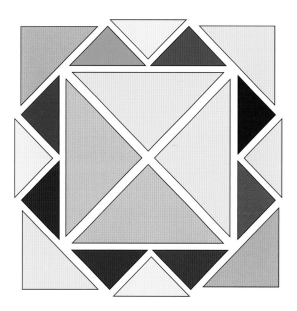

2. Sew the light and dark print B triangles together in sets of three as shown. Press the seam allowances toward the dark print triangles.

3. Sew a B triangle set from Step 2 to each of the A triangles as shown. Press the seam allowances toward the A triangles.

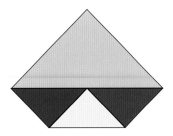

4. Sew the A/B units from Step 3 together in pairs; press the seam allowances in opposite directions. Sew the pairs together as shown. Press the seam allowances in one direction.

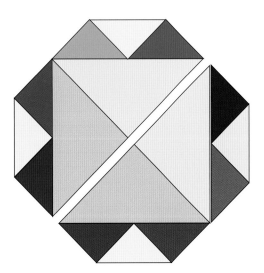

5. Join the light print C triangles to complete the block as shown. Press the seam allowances toward the C triangles. Repeat Steps 1-5 to make a total of 6 A Blocks.

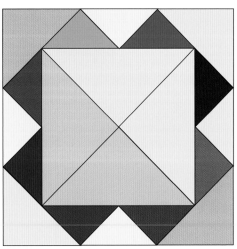

Make 6 A blocks

6. For Block B, arrange 4 light print A triangles, 8 light print B triangles, 4 dark print B triangles, and 4 dark print C triangles as shown. Sew the pieces together, following Steps 2-5 to make 12 B blocks.

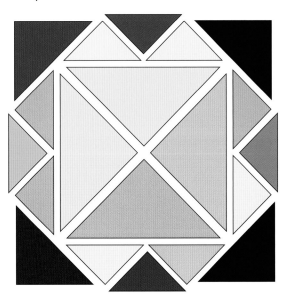

7. Sew the light and dark print B triangles together in sets of three as shown. Press the seam allowances toward the dark print triangles.

8. Sew a B triangle set from Step 2 to each of the A triangles as shown. Press the seam allowances toward the A triangles.

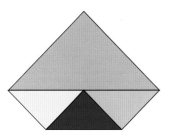

9. Sew the A/B units from Step 3 together in pairs; press the seam allowances in opposite directions. Sew the pairs together as shown. Press the seam allowances in one direction.

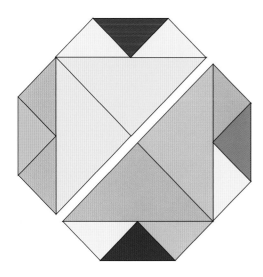

10. Join the light print C triangles to complete the block as shown. Press the seam allowances toward the C triangles. Repeat Steps 1-5 to make a total of 6 B Blocks.

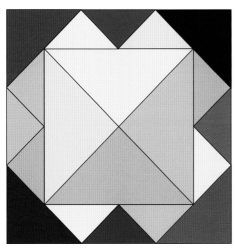

Make 6 B blocks

11. For a half-block, arrange 2 light print A triangles, 4 light print B triangles, 4 dark print B triangles, and 1 light print C triangle as shown. Refer to Steps 2-5 to make ten half-blocks, sewing the B triangles together in sets of 4.

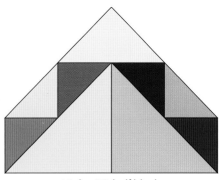

Make 10 half-blocks

12. For a quarter-block, arrange 1 light print A triangle, 3 light print B triangles, and 2 dark print B triangles as shown. Refer to Steps 2-3 to make 4 quarter-blocks, sewing the B triangles together in sets of 5.

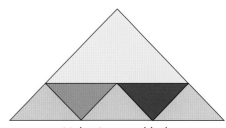

Make 4 quarter-blocks

Assembling the Quilt Top

1. Lay out the 6 A blocks, twelve B blocks, ten half-blocks, and 4 quarter-blocks on a large flat surface as shown.

2. Referring to the diagram on page 88, sew the blocks, half-blocks, and quarter-blocks together into diagonal rows. Press the seam allowances of each row to one side, alternating the direction with each row. Sew the rows together to complete the quilt top. Press the seam allowances in one direction.

Finishing the Quilt

1. Sew together the 38" x 58" backing rectangles along one long edge, using a 1/2" seam allowance. Press the seam allowances open.

2. Layer the pieced backing, the batting, and the quilt top. Baste the layers together and hand- or machine-quilt as desired.

3. Use diagonal seams to sew the 2-1/2"-wide dark green print binding strips together to make one long strip. Sew binding to the edges of the quilt.

4. Trim the extra batting and backing even with the edges of the quilt top. Turn the binding over the edge to the back and hand- or machine-sew in place.

Fields & Streams Quilt

nautical alphabet

Finished Size:
52-1/2" x 60-1/2"

Block Size:
6" square

Materials
1-1/8 yards of yellow fabric for blocks and binding

1 yard of red fabric for blocks and middle border

1 yard of white fabric for blocks and outer border

1 yard of black fabric for blocks, inner border, and outer border

1 yard of light blue fabric for sashing

5/8 yard of dark blue fabric for blocks

3-1/4 yards of backing fabric

58" x 66" piece of batting

Lightweight paper-back fusible web

Lightweight tear-away stabilizer

Yardages are for 44/45"-wide fabrics.

Cutting measurements include 1/4" seam allowances.

Cutting Instructions

From yellow fabric, cut:
(1) 6-1/2" x 42" strip.
　From the strip, cut:
　(2) 6-1/2" squares for Blocks I and Q.
　(1) 3-1/2" x 6-1/2" rectangle for Block K.
　(2) 2-1/4" x 6-1/2" rectangles for Block D.
　(4) 1-1/2" x 6-1/2" strips for Blocks G and R.
(7) 2-1/4" x 42" binding strips.
(5) 1-1/2" x 42" strips.
　From the strips, cut:
　(5) 1-1/2" x 15" for Block Y.
　(2) 1-1/2" x 3" rectangle for Block R.
(1) 7-1/4" square for Block Z.
　Cut the square into quarters diagonally to make 4 triangles.
(1) 6-7/8" square for Block O.
　Cut the square in half diagonally to make 2 triangles.
(2) 3-1/2" squares for Block L.

From red fabric, cut:
(2) 6-1/2" x 42" strips.
　From the strips, cut:
　(5) 6-1/2" squares for Block B and corner blocks.
　(2) 3-1/2" x 6-1/2" rectangles for Blocks E and H.
　(1) 2-1/2" x 6-1/2" rectangle for Block T.
　(1) 1-3/4" x 6-1/2" rectangle for Block C.
(8) 1-1/2" x 42" strips.
　From the strips, cut:
　(5) 1-1/2" x 15" strips for Block Y. Reserve extra for middle border.
(1) 7-1/4" square for Block Z.
　Cut the square into quarters diagonally to make 4 triangles.
(1) 6-7/8" square for Block O.
　Cut the square in half diagonally to make 2 triangles.
(2) 3-7/8" squares for Block F.
　Cut the squares in half diagonally to make a total of 4 triangles.
(2) 3-1/2" squares for Block U.
(4) 3" squares for Block R.

From white fabric, cut:

(1) 6-1/2" x 42" strip.
 From the strip, cut:
 (2) 6-1/2" squares for Blocks S and V.
 (2) 3-1/2" x 6-1/2" rectangles for Blocks A and H.
 (2) 2-1/2" x 6-1/2" rectangles for Blocks J and T.
 (2) 1-5/8" x 6-1/2" strips for Block C.
(1) 2" x 42" strip.
 From the strip, cut:
 (12) 2" squares for Blocks N and X.
(9) 1-1/2" x 42" outer border strips.
(2) 3-7/8" squares for Block F.
 Cut the squares in half diagonally to make 4 triangles.
(2) 3-1/2" squares for Block U.

From black fabric, cut:

(14) 1-1/2" x 42" inner and outer border strips.
(1) 7-1/4" square for Block Z.
 Cut the square into quarters diagonally to make 4 triangles.
(2) 3-1/2" squares for Block L.

From light blue fabric, cut:

(14) 2-1/2" x 42" strips.

Note: *If your fabric is at least 42-1/2" wide, you will only need 13 strips.*
 From the strips, cut:
 (36) 2-1/2" x 6-1/2" vertical sashing strips. Reserve extra for horizontal sashing strips.

From dark blue fabric, cut:

(2) 6-1/2" x 42" strips.
 From the strips, cut:
 (3) 6-1/2" squares for Blocks M, P and W.
 (4) 3-1/2" x 6-1/2" rectangles for Blocks A, E, K, and X.
 (1) 3" x 6-1/2" rectangle for Block D.
 (3) 2-1/2" x 6-1/2" rectangles for Blocks J and T.
 (2) 1-3/4" x 6-1/2" strips for Block C.
 (3) 1-1/2" x 6-1/2" strips for Block G.
(1) 7-1/4" square for Block Z.
 Cut the square into quarters diagonally to make 4 triangles.

(2) 2" x 3-1/2" rectangles for Block X.
(8) 2" squares for Block N.

From backing fabric, cut:

(2) 33-1/2" x 58" backing rectangles.

Preparing the Appliqué Pieces

1. Using the appliqué templates on pages 98 - 99, trace the X and triangle shapes twice onto the paper side of the fusible web. In addition, draw a 3-1/2"-diameter circle, a 3-1/2" square, (2) 3" squares, and a 1-1/2" square on the paper side of the web. Cut out the shapes, leaving a scant 1/4" around the outside of each shape.

2. Following the manufacturer's directions, fuse one X and the 1-1/2" square web shapes on the wrong side of the red fabric. Fuse (1) 3" square web shape on the wrong side of the dark blue fabric and the 3-1/2"-diameter circle web shape on the wrong side of the black fabric. Fuse the remaining web shapes onto the wrong side of the white fabric. Cut out each appliqué shape on the drawn lines. Remove the paper from the fusible web.

Assembling the Flag Blocks

1. For Block A, sew together a 3-1/2" x 6-1/2" white and 3-1/2" x 6-1/2" dark blue rectangle. Press the seam allowances toward the dark blue rectangle. Position a white triangle appliqué piece on the dark blue half of the block, aligning the long edge of the triangle with the long raw edge of the blue rectangle as shown; fuse in place.

2. For Block B, position a white triangle appliqué piece on a 6-1/2" red square, aligning the long edge of the triangle with

one raw edge of the red square as shown; fuse in place.

3. For Block C, sew together a 1-3/4" x 6-1/2" red rectangle, (2) 1-5/8" x 6-1/2" white strips, and (2) 1-3/4" x 6-1/2" dark blue strips as shown. Press the seam allowances away from the white strips.

4. For Block D, sew together a 3" x 6-1/2" dark blue rectangle and (2) 2-1/4" x 6-1/2" yellow rectangles as shown. Press the seam allowances toward the dark blue rectangle.

5. For Block E, sew together a 3-1/2" x 6-1/2" red rectangle and a 3-1/2" x 6-1/2" dark blue rectangle as shown. Press the seam allowances in one direction.

6. For Block F, sew together 4 red and 4 white triangles cut from the 3-7/8" squares as shown. Press the seam allowances toward the red triangles.

Arrange the half-square triangles as shown. Sew the half-square triangles together into rows; press the seam allowances in opposite directions. Sew the rows together to complete the block. Press the seam allowances in one direction.

7. For Block G, sew together (3) 1-1/2" x 6-1/2" dark blue strips and (3) 1-1/2" x 6-1/2" yellow strips as shown. Press the seam allowances toward the blue strips.

8. For Block H, sew together a 3-1/2" x 6-1/2" red rectangle and a 3-1/2" x 6-1/2" white rectangle as shown. Press the seam allowances in one direction.

9. For Block I, center a black circle appliqué piece on a 6-1/2" yellow square as shown; fuse in place.

10. For Block J, sew together (2) 2-1/2" x 6-1/2" dark blue rectangles and (1) 2-1/2" x 6-1/2" white rectangle as shown. Press seam allowances toward the dark blue rectangles.

11. For Block K, sew together a 3-1/2" x 6-1/2" yellow rectangle and a 3-1/2" x 6-1/2" dark blue rectangle as shown. Press the seam allowances in one direction.

12. For Block L, arrange (2) 3-1/2" yellow squares and (2) 3-1/2" black squares as shown. Sew the squares together into rows; press the seam allowances in opposite directions. Sew the rows together to complete the block. Press the seam allowances in one direction.

13. For Block M, center a white X appliqué piece on a 6-1/2" dark blue square as shown; fuse in place.

14. For Block N, arrange (8) 2" dark blue squares and (8) 2" white squares as shown. Sew the squares together into rows; press the seam allowances toward the dark blue squares. Sew the rows together to complete the block. Press the seam allowances in one direction.

15. For Block O, sew together 1 red and 1 yellow triangle cut from the 6-7/8" squares as shown. Press the seam allowances toward the red triangle.

16. For Block P, center a white 3-1/2" square appliqué piece on a 6-1/2" dark blue square as shown; fuse in place.

17. For Block R, sew (4) 3" red squares and (2) 1-1/2" x 3" yellow strips together into rows as shown. Press the seam allowances toward the red squares. Attach the rows with a 1-1/2" x 6-1/2" yellow strip as shown. Press the seam allowances toward the yellow strip.

18. For Block S, center a blue 3" square appliqué piece on a 6-1/2" white square as shown; fuse in place.

19. For Block T, sew together a 2-1/2" x 6-1/2" red rectangle, a 2-1/2" x 6-1/2" white rectangle, and a 2-1/2" x 6-1/2" dark blue rectangle as shown. Press the seam allowances away from the white rectangle.

20. For Block U, arrange (2) 3-1/2" red squares and (2) 3-1/2" white squares as shown. Sew the squares together into rows; press the seam allowances in opposite directions. Sew the rows together to complete the block. Press the seam allowances in one direction.

21. For Block V, center a red X appliqué piece on a 6-1/2" white square as shown; fuse in place.

22. For Block W, center a white 3" square appliqué piece on a 6-1/2" blue square and a red 1-1/2" square red appliqué piece on the white square as shown. Fuse in place.

23. For Block X, sew together (4) 2" white squares and (2) 2" x 3-1/2" dark blue rectangles in columns as shown. Press the seam allowances away from the white squares. Attach the columns with a 3-1/2" x 6-1/2" dark blue rectangle as shown. Press the seam allowances toward the dark blue rectangle.

24. For Block Y, sew the (5) 1-1/2" x 15" red strips and (5) 1-1/2" x 15" yellow strips as shown. Cut a 6-1/2" square block from the pieced strips.

25. For Block Z, sew together 1 red, 1 yellow, 1 blue, and 1 black triangle cut from the 7-1/4" squares in pairs as shown. Press the seam allowances toward the black and blue triangles. Sew the pairs together to complete the block. Press the seam allowances in one direction.

26. For all appliquéd blocks, cut a piece of tear-away stabilizer slightly larger than each appliquéd shape. Place the stabilizer on the wrong side of the block. Using matching thread and a satin zigzag stitch, stitch along the edges of each appliqué piece; do not stitch the edges that align with the raw edges of the block. Carefully remove the stabilizer after stitching.

Assembling the Quilt Center

1. Sew together the 8 remaining 2-1/2"-wide light blue strips to make one long strip. From the strip, cut (7) 2-1/2" x 42-1/2" sashing strips.

2. Lay out the assembled flag blocks, a 6-1/2" yellow square for Block Q, (4) 6-1/2" red corner blocks, (36) 2-1/2" x 6-1/2" sashing strips, and (7) 2-1/2" x 42-1/2" sashing strips on a large flat surface as shown.

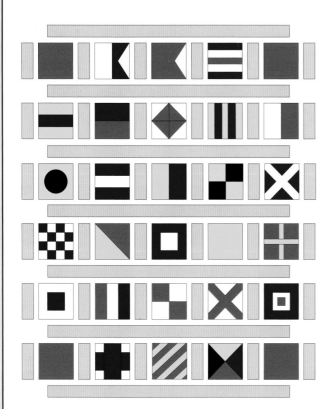

3. Sew the flag blocks, corner blocks, and 2-1/2" x 6-1/2" sashing strips together in horizontal rows. Press the seam allowances toward the sashing strips.

4. Sew the rows together with the 2-1/2" x 42-1/2" sashing strips. Add a sashing strip to the top of the first row and the bottom of the last row to complete the quilt center. Press the seam allowances toward the sashing strips.

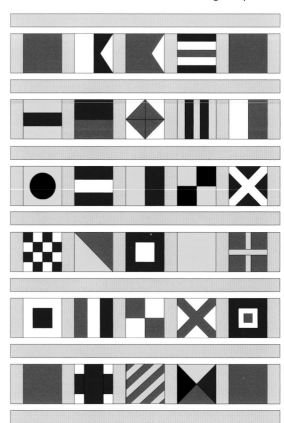

Adding the Borders

1. Sew together (5) 1-1/2" x 42" black border strips to make one long strip. From the strip, cut (2) 1-1/2" x 42-1/2" top and bottom inner border strips and (2) 1-1/2" x 52-1/2" side inner border strips.

2. Sew the 42-1/2" lengths to the top and bottom edges of the quilt center. Press the seam allowances toward the inner border. Sew the 52-1/2" lengths to the left and right edges of the quilt center. Press the seams toward the inner border.

3. Sew together the five remaining 1-1/2" x 42" red strips to make one long strip. From this strip, cut (2) 1-1/2" x 44-1/2" top and bottom middle border strips and (2) 1-1/2" x 54-1/2" side middle border strips.

4. Sew the 44-1/2" lengths to the top and bottom edges of the inner border. Press the seam allowances toward the middle border. Sew the 54-1/2" lengths to the left and right edges of the quilt center. Press the seams toward the middle border.

5. To make the piano key outer border, sew together (3) 1-1/2"-wide black strips and (3) 1-1/2"-wide white strips to make one strip set as shown. Press the seam allowances toward the black strips. Repeat to make 2 additional strip sets. Cut 3-1/2"-wide segments from each strip set as shown for a total of 36 segments.

3-1/2"   Make 36 Segments

6. Sew together 9 segments to make one side outer border, continuing the black/white pattern. Press the seam allowances toward the black "keys". Repeat to make a second

side outer border. Sew these to the left and right edges of the middle border. Press the seam allowances toward the middle border.

7. Sew together 9 segments for the top outer border, again continuing the black/white pattern. Use your seam ripper to remove two "keys" from the last segment so you have a total of 52 "keys". Repeat to make the bottom outer border. Sew these to the top and bottom edges of the middle border. Press the seam allowances toward the middle border.

Finishing the Quilt

1. Sew together the 33-1/2" x 58" backing rectangles along one long edge, using a 1/2" seam allowance. Press the seam allowances open.

2. Layer the pieced backing, the batting, and the quilt top. Baste the layers together and hand- or machine-quilt as desired.

3. Use diagonal seams to sew the 2-1/4"-wide yellow binding strips together to make one long strip. Sew binding to the edges of the quilt.

4. Trim the extra batting and backing even with the edges of the quilt top. Turn the binding over the edge to the back and hand- or machine-sew in place.

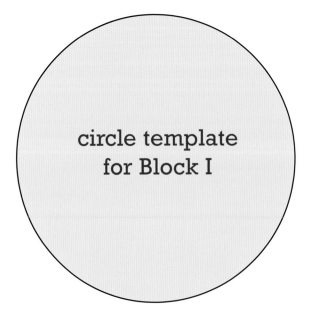

circle template
for Block I

triangle template
for Blocks A & B

X template
for Blocks M & V

Nautical Alphabet

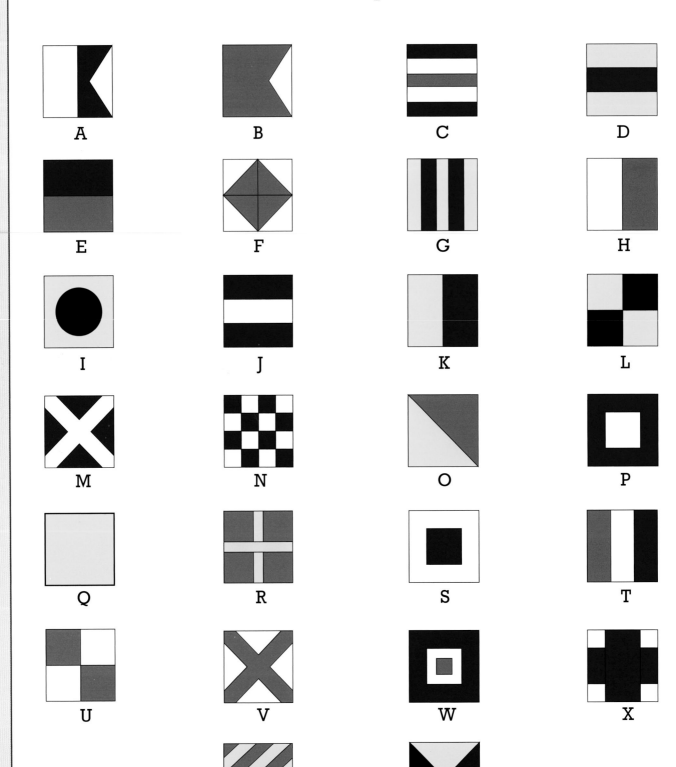

Nautical Alphabet Quilt

indian meadows

Finished Size:
63-1/2" x 63-1/2"

Block Size
17-1/2"

Materials

1-1/4 yards of cream medium-print fabric for center square, inner border, and middle border

1-1/4 yards of turquoise print fabric for blocks, inner border, and outer border

1-1/8 yards of multi-color fabric for setting triangles and corner triangles

1 yard of cream small-print fabric for blocks

3/4 yard of brown print fabric for middle border and binding

5/8 yard of brown/green print fabric for middle border

4 yards of backing fabric

70" x 70" piece of batting

Yardages are for 44/45"-wide fabrics.

Cutting measurements include 1/4" seam allowances.

Cutting Instructions

From cream medium-print fabric, cut:
- (1) 18" center square.
- (7) 3-1/2" x 42" strips.
  From the strips, cut:
  (16) 3-1/2" squares; reserve extra for inner border.

From turquoise print fabric, cut:
- (1) 7-7/8" x 42" strip.
  From the strip, cut
  (4) 7-7/8" half-square triangle squares.
- (2) 4-3/8" x 42" strips.
  From the strips, cut:
  (12) 4-3/8" half-square triangle squares.
- (3) 4" x 42" strips.

From the strips, cut (28) 4" squares.
- (1) 3-1/2" x 42" strip.
  From the strip, cut:
  (4) 3-1/2" squares.
- (6) 1-1/2" x 42" outer border strips.

From multi-color fabric, cut:
- (2) 18-3/8" squares; cut the squares in half diagonally to make 4 setting triangles.
- (1) 18-3/4" square; cut the square into quarters diagonally to make 4 corner triangles.

From cream small-print fabric, cut:
- (1) 7-7/8" x 42" strip.
  From the strip, cut:
  (4) 7-7/8" half-square triangle squares.
- (2) 4-3/8" x 42" strips.
  From the strips, cut:
  (12) 4-3/8" half-square triangle squares.
- (4) 4" x 42" strips.
  From the strips, cut:
  (16) 4" x 7-1/2" rectangles.
  (8) 4" squares.

From brown print fabric, cut:
(2) 3-1/2" x 42" strips.
From the strips, cut:
(8) 3-1/2" x 6-1/2" rectangles.
(4) 3-1/2" squares.
(7) 2-1/2" x 42" binding strips.

From brown/green print fabric, cut:
(5) 3-1/2" x 42" middle border strips.
Note: *If your fabric is at least 43-1/2" wide, you will only need 4 strips.*

From backing fabric, cut:
(2) 35-1/2" x 70" backing rectangles.

Painting the Center Square
1. Copy the templates on pages 108 - 109. The sunburst template at 100% and the eagle at 140%. Cut the templates out.

2. Place the paper side of freezer paper on top of photocopied paper pattern; so the iron does not smear the ink on the copy. With the waxy side down, iron the freezer paper to the blank side of the copied paper templates. Freezer paper is available at grocery stores in the paper products aisle.

3. Place the eagle template in the center of the fabric square and iron to hold in place. Using a water soluble marker trace around the eagle template. Remove the template from the center square.

4. Place the sunburst template in the center of the eagle and iron to hold in place. Using a water soluble marker trace around the sunburst template. Remove the template.

5. With a bronze metallic fabric marker trace the shape of the eagle with as thick a line as desired. Trace the sunburst with a gold metallic fabric marker.

6. Following the manufacturer's directions use paintstiks to paint the eagle and sunburst as desired.

Trapunto the Eagle Design
1. Cut pieces of quilt batting at least 1" to 2" larger than the size of the quilting designs you wish to stuff.

2. Mark the quilting designs on your wallhanging top, using a water-soluble marker for light fabrics or a chalk pencil for dark fabrics. Place two pieces of batting underneath a Trapunto area on the wallhanging top and pin in place. Use open safety pins because they are easier to remove than straight pins.

3. Thread your machine with water-soluble thread on top and a light-weight cotton thread in the bobbin. Use a thread color to match the batting. Loosen the top tension. Stitch the Trapunto area of the quilting design. Be careful to keep the two layers of batting flat. Some battings slide more easily under the needle than others.

4. Cut away the batting in the areas not intended to be stuffed.

Making the Half-Square Triangles

1. Draw a diagonal line on the wrong side of (12) 4-3/8" cream small-print squares as shown.

Make 12

2. With right sides together, layer the 4-3/8" cream small-print squares on (12) 4-3/8" turquoise squares. Sew 1/4" from each side of the drawn lines as shown.

3. Cut on the drawn line between the stitching as shown. Press the seam allowances toward the turquoise fabric. Check to be sure your 24 cream/turquoise half-square triangles each measure 4" square; trim if necessary.

Make 24

4. Repeat Steps 1-3 with (4) 7-7/8" cream small-print squares and (4) 7-7/8" turquoise squares to make 8 cream/turquoise half-square triangles each measuring 7-1/2" square; trim if necessary.

Making the Flying Geese Units

1. Draw a diagonal line on the wrong side of (24) 4" turquoise squares as shown.

Make 24

2. With right sides together, align a 4" turquoise square with the right end of a 4" x 7-1/2" cream small-print rectangle as shown. Sew on the drawn line and trim the seam allowances to 1/4". Press the seam

allowances toward the turquoise triangle. Repeat to make 16 Flying Geese half-units.

Make 16

3. Sew another 4" turquoise square to the opposite end of 8 of the rectangles in the same manner to make Flying Geese units as shown. Check to be sure the unit measures 4" x 7-1/2". You should have a total of 8 turquoise/cream Flying Geese units and 8 turquoise/cream Flying Geese half-units for the blocks.

Make 8

4. Repeat Steps 1-3 with (16) 3-1/2" cream medium-print squares and (8) 3-1/2" x 6-1/2" brown print rectangles to make 8 cream/brown Flying Geese units for the middle border as shown.

Make 16

Make 8

Assembling the Blocks

1. Arrange 1 Flying Geese unit, 1 Flying Geese half-unit, one small cream/turquoise half-square triangle and (1) 4" cream small-print square as shown. Sew the pieces together in rows, pressing the seam allowances toward the square and the Flying Geese half-unit. Sew the rows together. Press the seam allowances in one direction.

2. Sew a large cream/turquoise half-square triangle to the left edge of the Flying Geese units as shown to complete the top section of the block. Press the seam allowances toward the half-square triangle. Repeat Steps 1-2 for the bottom section of the block.

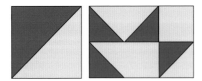

3. Arrange 4 small cream/turquoise half-square triangles and (1) 4" turquoise square as shown. Sew the pieces together in a row. Press the seam allowances in the direction needed to create the least bulk.

4. Use the row to sew the top and bottom sections together as shown, completing one block. Press the seam allowances away from the row. Repeat Steps 1-4 to make a total of 4 blocks.

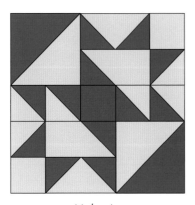

Make 4

Assembling the Wallhanging Center

1. Lay out the painted center square, the 4 blocks, 4 multi-color setting triangles and 4 multi-color corner triangles on a large flat surface as shown.

2. Sew the center square, blocks, and the setting triangles together into diagonal rows, pressing the seam allowances toward the center square and setting triangles. Sew the rows together to complete the wallhanging center. Press the seam allowances in one direction.

Adding the Borders

1. Sew together the remaining 3-1/2" x 42" cream medium-print strips to make one long strip. From the strip, cut (4) 49-1/2" inner border strips. Sew strips to the left and right edges of the wallhanging center. Press the seam allowances toward the inner border.

2. Sew a 3-1/2" turquoise square to each end of the two remaining inner border strips. Press the seam allowances toward the inner border strips. Sew these pieced inner border strips to the remaining edges of the wallhanging center. Press the seam allowances toward the inner border.

3. Sew together the (5) 3-1/2" x 42" brown/green print middle border strips to make one long strip. From the strip, cut (4) 43-1/2" middle border strips.

4. Sew a cream/brown Flying Geese unit to each end of the 43-1/2"-long middle border strips as shown. Sew pieced strips to the left and right edges of the inner border. Press the seam allowances toward the inner border.

5. Sew a 3-1/2" brown print square to the ends of the two remaining middle border strips as shown. Press the seam allowances toward the squares. Sew these pieced strips to the remaining edges of the inner border. Press the seam allowances toward the inner border.

6. Sew together the (6) 1-1/2" x 42" turquoise outer border strips to make one long strip. From the strip, cut (2) 61-1/2" lengths and (2) 63-1/2" lengths. Sew the 61-1/2" lengths to the left and right edges of the middle border. Press the seam allowances

toward the outer border. Sew the remaining lengths to the top and bottom edges of the middle border. Press the seam allowances toward the outer border.

Finishing the Wallhanging

1. Sew together the 35-1/2" x 70" backing rectangles along one long edge, using a 1/2" seam allowance. Press the seam allowances open.

2. Layer the pieced backing, the batting, and the wallhanging top. Baste the layers together and hand- or machine-quilt as desired.

3. Use diagonal seams to sew the 2-1/2"-wide brown print binding strips together to make one long strip. Sew binding to the edges of the wallhanging.

4. Trim the extra batting and backing even with the edges of the wallhanging top. Turn the binding over the edge to the back and hand- or machine-sew in place.

sunburst template

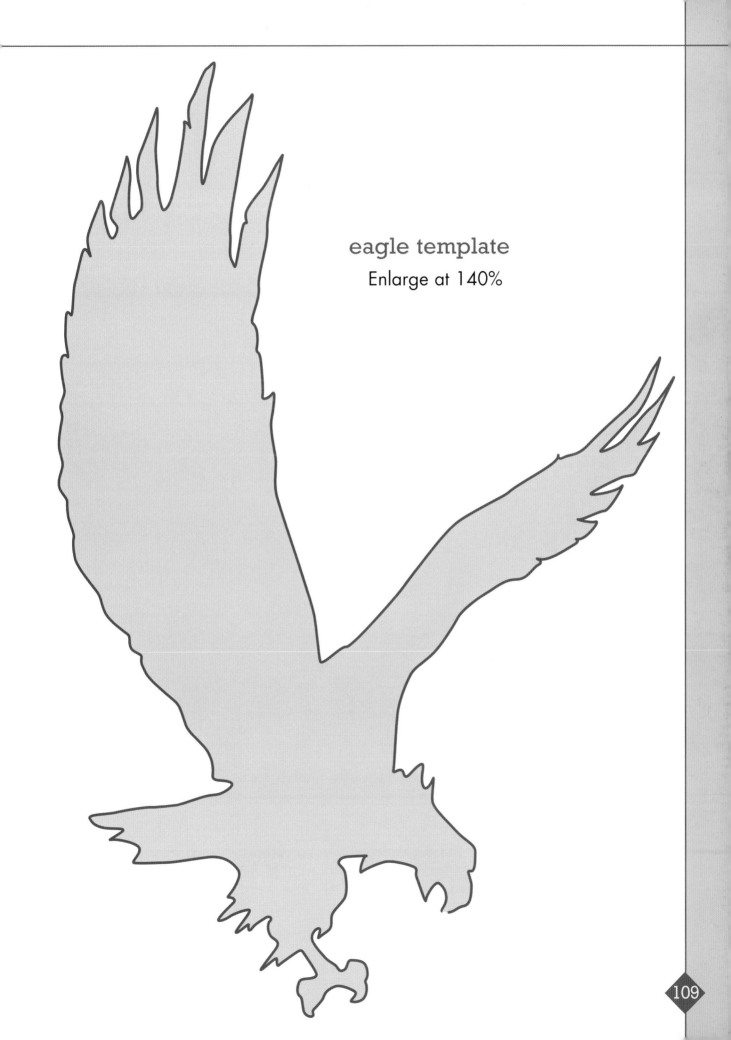

eagle template

Enlarge at 140%

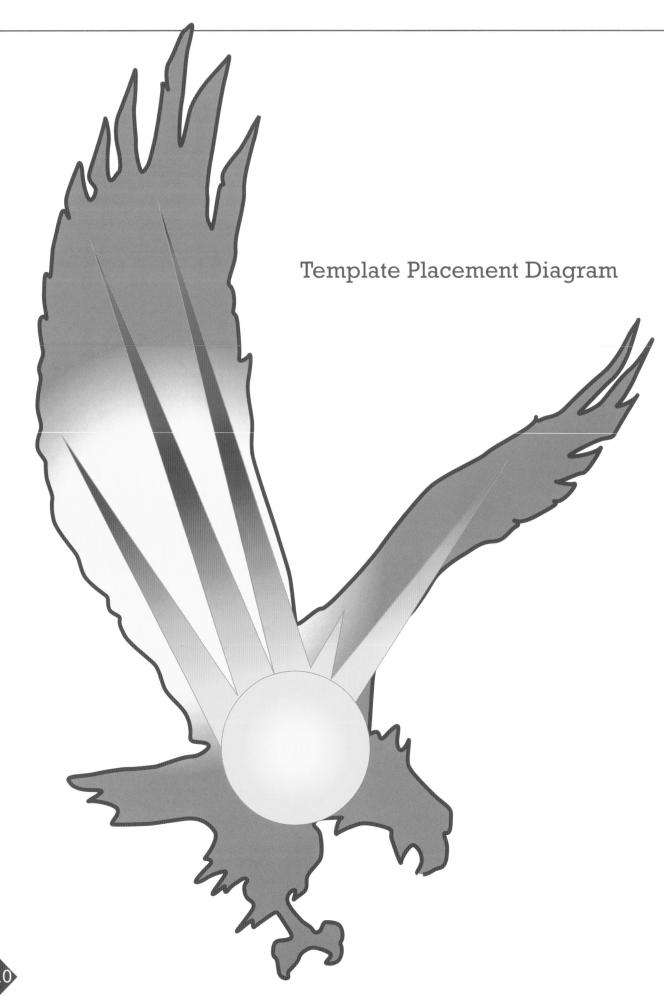

Template Placement Diagram

Indian Meadows Wallhanging

Quilts for Men

from Crib to Dorm to Den

Quilt Designers, Piecers & Quilters

Baby Pinwheel—by Penny Haren

Buggy Nights—designed by Janet Pittman; made by Mary Cecil,
Kristine Peterson, and Janet Pittman

Sheriff Billy—designed and made by Penny Haren;
quilted by Cheryl Lorence

Beach Quilt—by Janet Pittman

Magic Cape—designed and made by Margaret Sindelar

Bachelor's Wheel—designed and quilted by Shirley Harrison;
made by Abigail Livingood

Huddle-Up—designed and made by Jeri Simon; quilted by
Flying Needle Quilting of West Des Moines, IA

Patriot Games—designed by Sonja Moen and Vicki Lynn Oehlke of
WillowBerry Lane; pieced by Vonnie Erickstad; quilted by Barb Simons

Tee Time—by Cyndee Davis

Fields & Streams—by Shirley Harrison

Nautical Alphabet—designed and made by Sue Voegtlin;
quilted by Lynn Witzenburg

Indian Meadows—designed and painted by Laurel Albright;
made by Kathy Wunder; quilted by Lynn Witzenburg